COPTIC ORTHODOX PATRIARCHATE

See of St. Mark

Contemplations on

THE SERMON ON THE MOUNT

BY

HIS HOLINESS POPE SHENOUDA III

Title   : Contemplations on the Sermon On The Mount.
Author   : H. H. Pope Shenouda III.
Translated by: Mr. Aziz Gharbawi - B.A. Classics.
Illustrated by : Sister Sawsan.
Edition   : The First - September 1991.
Typesetting   : J. C. Center. - Heliopolis - Cairo.
Press   : Dar El Tebaa El Kawmia.
Legal Deposit: 9768/1990
Revised   : COEPA 1997

3

H.H. Pope Shenouda III
117th Pope and Patriarch of Alexandria and
the See of St Mark

CONTENTS

THE STORY OF THIS BOOK

This book "The Sermon On The Mount" is the fruit of sixteen lectures delivered by me when I was The Bishop responsible for Education.

At first, the lectures were delivered in St. Mark's Hall in Abba Roweis Monastery. When the hall became too small and could not hold the great numbers of the congregation, the meeting was held in the courtyard of the Theological College.

These lectures were delivered between Friday the 30th of June and Friday the 13th of October 1967, at the time when the foundations of the great cathedral were being laid.

At the end of February 1969, I began lecturing there.

This book includes the Beatitudes and the sayings of The Lord: *"You are the salt of the earth." "You are the light of the world."*

I'd like to pause at this point in the first part of our contemplations on the Sermon on the Mount and begin the second part in a subsequent volume with the words of our Lord *"Do not think that I have come to abolish the Law or the Prophets; I have not come to abolish them but to fulfil them."*

I have returned to the contemplation of these subjects with you on Wednesdays. May The Lord support me to publish them for you, after completion. God Willing.

Shenouda III

PREFACE

The Mount:

Some people say that the insights of the "Sermon on the Mount" are the statutes and the regulations of Christianity and we add that they are the highest instructions ever known to man.

With these teachings, Our Lord Jesus Christ spoke to all people. This proves that perfection can be offered to all human beings and that everyone has, in his inmost soul, the readiness to listen to these valuable instructions and highest principles, to love them and be fully content in them, whatever obstacles meet his will to listen.

It was fitting that these heavenly words should be delivered from the top of a high mountain in order that the audience, during their ascent, might elevate their souls to the standard with which they would be able to understand such instructions.

Undoubtedly, he who sits on a mountain sees the things on earth as very small and tiny.

We must not forget that the laws of 'The Old Testament' had been given from a mountain top where the people

11

could perceive the Most High in the Heavens, His greatness and His dignity.

It was therefore appropriate for the Lord to offer New Testament law to the people from a mountain top to remind them of Mount Sinai.

In his epistle to the Hebrews, **Saint Paul the apostle, made a comparison between** the two mountains. He said "*For You have not come to a mountain that may be touched and that burned with fire; and to blackness and darkness and tempest , and the sound of trumpet and the voice words so that those who heard it begged that the word should not be spoken to them, ...*

But you have come to Mount Zion, and to city of the living God, the heavenly Jerusalem ... and to Jesus the mediator of a new covenant" (Heb 12 :18 - 24).

Contrary to the New Testament, the laws of the Old Testament were given in a way which filled a person with fear, such that Moses the prophet, said "I am trembling with fear."

The Lord Jesus Christ used to speak gently. In the beginning of His blessings He was praising meekness. The people neither feared fire, fog nor earthquakes. They did not need a mediator like Moses to convey God's word to them. The Lord was among His sons, speaking to them as a loving father. He spoke to them so effectively that it was said "*The people were astonished at His teaching, for He taught as one having authority, and not as the scribes*" (Matt 7:29).

12

It was good that the Lord spoke to them from the top of a mountain where there was nothing to disturb their senses. This is why they concentrated their thoughts on what the Lord was saying.

He spoke to them where there were no obstacles, away from the town with its brilliance, amusement, enjoyment, anxiety and crowds. No worries or entertainment, whether at home or at work, could take them away. But here is God alone. Nothing could hinder them or keep their senses and thoughts away. **Mar Isaac was correct when he said: "A mere look at the wilderness can mortify all worldly desires in man's heart".**

This is why Jesus used to take the people to remote and deserted places. (Luke 9:10).

Sometimes He took them to the sea-shore or around a lake. The most important thing was to keep them far from materialism and worldly affairs, so that they might devote themselves to Him, as the Lord had told Abram to leave his country, his people and his father's household. (Gen 12: 1).

It was also good that the crowds followed Jesus Christ towards the mount.

Jesus' attractive personality, His instructions, the testimony of John the Baptist, the talks of His disciples who had followed Him and some of His miracles attracted all the people.

Jesus' reputation as "The man of the multitudes" remained with Him till the time of His crucifixion. He was continually

13

followed by thousands and surrounded with crowds everywhere.

The elders spoke of Him and said *"Look how the whole world has gone after Him!"* (John 12:19).

It was also said about Him *"All the people were very attentive to hear Him."* (Luke 19:48).

He took them to the mountain as He had with Moses in the past.

In the past, Elijah had lived his life on a mountain - Karmal Mountain - Even Elisha and the sons of the prophets lived there. John the Baptist lived his life in the wilderness as Elijah had done.

Much time is needed to discuss the effect of mountains and wilderness on the life of saints, monks and hermits who practised the life of prayers and contemplation.

The mountain became an influence in the life of Jesus Himself.

It was said about Him in "Song of Songs" *"Behold! He comes, leaping upon the mountains, skipping upon the hills"* (Song 2:8).

After His baptism, Jesus spent forty days praying on a mountain.

After the Spirit of God had descended like a dove and enlightened Jesus before He began His service, there was a time in which He lived in retreat and seclusion.

During that period He laid down the fundamental principles of the program of His service.

These principles seemed clear when Jesus was face to face with the devil on this mountain which was afterwards called "The Mount of Temptation".

From the Mount of Temptation to the Mount of the Sermon, then to the Mount of Olives.

The Mount of Olives was one of the places pleasing to Jesus and loved by Him. It was the place of His retreats which He continually visited, spending His time in contemplation and prayers and enjoying the best relationship with "The Father".

How beautiful were the words of John were when he wrote *"And everyone went to his own house. But Jesus went to the Mount of Olives".* (John 7:53, 8:1).

The Garden of Gethsemane was one of the beloved places He experienced His spiritual struggles for our sake. This happened immediately before He was arrested and before He would go to another mount during His journey to the Cross, leaping across the mountains.

That is the Mount of Golgotha where the Lord recorded the greatest story of love and self-sacrifice in order to save humanity.

On this mountain, the Lord's blood was shed. On this mountain, hung on the cross, He spoke His seven famous sayings.

On the same mountain, He forgave the sins of both the thief who was crucified at His right hand and of all humankind. Indeed, it is the mountain of suffering, affliction and love.

There is another mountain where the Lord gave the people a glimpse of His glory in order to strengthen their faith at the time of crucifixion.

This happened on Mount Tabor where the Transfiguration took place. This is why it was called **"The mountain of Transfiguration"** (Mark 9:2,3).

It is said that the Transfiguration occurred on a high mountain where Elijah and Moses appeared with Jesus Himself.

Both of these prophets had lived life on mountains or in the wilderness.

On this mountain God gave evidence in favour of Jesus saying *"This is My beloved Son, hear Him."* (Mark 9:7).

The Mount of Olives (one of His glorious mountains) is said to be the place from which Jesus was taken up into Heaven (Acts 1:9,12).

Because Jesus was fond of life on mountains, it was not strange for Him to deliver this famous sermon at the top of a mountain.

Even Matthew, the evangelist said about Him "*And seeing the multitude, He went up on a mountain, then He opened His mouth and taught them saying ...*" (Matt 5:1,2).

While on the mountain, the people could not see anything above them but the sky and the endless horizon. There was no material interference.

In such beautiful surroundings, under an endless sky, being away from materialism, they listened to the Lord when He opened His mouth and spoke to them.

He Opened His Mouth:

Perhaps some may ask: "What does the phrase 'He opened His mouth' mean?"

St. Augustine said "On this occasion, Jesus opened His own mouth because, on past occasions He used to open the mouths of the prophets in order that they might speak to the people..."

St. Paul the apostle said "*God ,who at various times and in different ways spoke in time past to the fathers by the prophets ... has in these last days spoken to us by His Son.*" (Heb 1:1,2).

It means that Jesus, on giving His sermon on the mount and on delivering other sermons, did not talk with us through the prophets but opened His own mouth and spoke to us.

St. John Chrysostom says "Jesus opened His mouth and spoke to the people because in the past years, He used to talk with them and teach them by giving instructive examples without opening His mouth.

Observations On The Contents Of The Sermon:

1. The sermon gives a comprehensive answer to those who teach that faith alone is sufficient, saying *Only, Have Faith"*

The whole sermon comprises of spiritual behaviour. No word was said about faith.

It is a discourse about the great virtues, purity of the heart, models of good manners, treatment of people, prayers, fasting, and the proper understanding of the Old Testament Commandments.

It ends with spiritual benefits ie. works and the verses: *"You will know them by their fruits. "Therefore whoever hears these sayings of Mine and does them, I will liken him to a wise man who built his house on the rock."* (Matt 7:16,24).

2. The Lord spoke about practical life. He mentioned nothing about rituals or practices and habits which the teachers of the Law used to discuss with the Jews. Thus His words affected the depths of people's hearts.

3. He spoke about perfection and conversed with all persons equally.

He talked with men, women, the elderly; people of different spiritual standards and ages.

He would lay before them what must be done. He helped them to ascend to the highest levels of glory.

He let each person act according to their own capabilities and the gifts they have.

He did not let them stop at a certain point on their spiritual journey and said to them *"Therefore, you shall be perfect, just as your Father in heaven is perfect."* (Matt 5:48).

4. On delivering the sermon on the mount, Jesus presented God as a heavenly Father.

He repeated the phrase "Your heavenly Father" and its synonyms about eleven times.

He also taught the people to pray saying "Our Father in Heaven...".

This assures the mutual understanding of love between God and man.

5. Many times, He also repeated the words *"The Kingdom"* and *"The Heavens."*

This is how He was able to change their passion for having earthly possessions, into that for a heavenly kingdom, high above the standard of the world and its materialism.

6. He did not address the subject of people's emotions or their paranoia.

He did not talk with them as one who wished to save them from Roman slavery, but said "*If anyone wants to sue you and take away your tunic, let him have your cloak also; and whoever compels you to go one mile, go with him two miles and not to resist an evil person*" (Matt 5:39-41).

He wished them to be adorned with inner purity and not with outer haughtiness.

O' my Lord! Who would find it easy to be devoted to You when You say "*Blessed are the poor*" or "*whoever slaps You on your right cheek, turn the other to him also*" or when You say "*Do not resist an evil person*"?

Perhaps He would respond "I did not come in order that someone might have devotion towards Me; I came to cleanse these hearts even if they would crucify Me. This is why there is no hesitation to begin My speech to them with this verse 'Blessed are the poor in spirit for theirs is the kingdom of heaven.' '.

In this article, we will speak about the first Beatitude of the sermon on the mount.

CHAPTER ONE
"Blessed Are The Poor In Spirit"

The Beatitudes:

The Lord Jesus Christ began His sermon with nine Beatitudes.

The word beatitude means *both* happiness and blessing together, not separately.

Some recent translations omit half of the meaning.

In some English texts, it is translated "*blessed*" while in others, the meaning is "*happy*". The correct translation joins the two meanings together.

Happiness is the fruit of being blessed. Within being blessed lies happiness.

Here the Lord Jesus Christ explains to the people the way that leads to both happiness and blessings.

God, Himself wants happiness for all His children. He begins His sermon with promising words "My sons; Come to Me, that the gates of happiness and blessings may open to you."

21

The Holy Gospel itself is cheerful news. The angel who announced Jesus' birth said to the shepherds "*I bring you good tidings of great joy which will be to all people*". (Luke 2:10).

Because happiness and blessedness mean different things to different people, Jesus Christ sat on the mount to explain to them the correct meaning of the word "beatitude".

He explained it with a new spiritual image which differed from that of society of the time, whether they were Romans or Jews.

It was not reasonable that the Romans - who governed with great authority and lived in splendour and arrogance - would agree that poverty in spirit could be the way to happiness.

Even the Jews, who were anxious to be free of Roman slavery could not accept the idea that poverty could be the path to blessedness.

The blessings given to Abraham were vast lands, numerous sons and great wealth.

God did not bless Abraham or his offspring with poverty but with a land flowing with milk and honey. (Ex 3:8).

This is why blessings were given to the people from the top of Mount Gerizim (Deut 27:11). It was said that "*The Lord will command the blessing on you in your storehouse and in all to which you set your hand and He will bless you in the land which The Lord your God is giving you.*" (Deut 28:8).

Here, The Lord explains the blessedness of the spirit, not of material things.

In the Old Testament, material blessings were symbols of spiritual ones in the New Testament.

It is believed that the people should have spiritual maturity to understand the spiritual meaning of blessings.

The first of these blessings is:

Spiritual Poverty:

It explained the way to avoid both Adam's sin and the sin of the devil.

Wishing to be great, the devil said "*I will be like the Most High*" (Is 14:14).

He tempted our first parents with the same sin, saying to them "*You will be like God.*" (Gen 3:5).

Having lost their spiritual poverty, they lost both their divine likeness and paradise.

Jesus came to rectify their first sin and to restore them to their original rank.

He said *"Blessed are the poor in spirit."* (Matt 5:3).

God, who made himself nothing, taking the very nature of a servant (Phil 2:7) does not like haughtiness.

It was said "*God resists the proud, but gives grace to the humble* " (James 4:6).

This is why He said in Isaiah "*But on this one will I look, on him trembles at My word*" (Is 66:2).

David, the prophet also said: "*Who is like the Lord our God, who dwells on high, who humbles Himself to behold , The thinks that are in the heavens and the earth? He raises the poor out of the dust and lifts the needy out of the ash heap; That He may seat him with princes, with the princes of His people*". (The heads of his nation) (Psalm112).

Spiritual poverty is clear and plain in the hymn of St. Mary "The Virgin "

She says "*For He has regarded the lowly state of His maidservant..., He has scattered the proud in the imagination of their hearts... He has put down the mighty from their thrones and exalted the lowly*" (Luke 1:48-52).

It is also a clear theme in David's life and in his psalms.

He speaks frequently of his spiritual poverty and of how he is in need of God. He continually, asks for His help and victory: Look at what he says to God! "*I am poor and needy, Make haste to me, O' God, You are my help and my deliverer, O' Lord, do not delay.*" (Psalm 69).

Oh Heavens! David, the great king, the general, the prophet and the judge says these words!

David, before whom great people, prophets and queens knelt down!! David, before whom the kings trembled. But before God, he is needy and poor. In his prayer to the Lord, David says: *"Bow down Your ear, O' Lord, hear me, for I am poor and needy."* (Psalm 85).

Although he was greatly praised by the people, he considered himself poor, needy and poor in spirit before God and miserable because of his spiritual struggles.

The holy history gives many examples of the poor loved by God.

Perhaps Abel is one of them. He was poor compared to his brother Cain, a tyrant and the first murderer on earth.

God defended Abel after his death and convicted his murderer and subjected him to the first curse to hit one of mankind. (Gen 4:11).

In the same way, God supported **Jacob** who was poor compared to his brother Esau.

Esau said *"I will kill my brother Jacob."* (Gen 27:4 1).

The Lord blessed Jacob, became incarnate through his offspring, and saved him from Esau.

God was with Joseph, whose brothers threw him in a well and sold him as a slave.

Joseph was accused unjustly by Potiphar's wife. In spite of his innocence, he was imprisoned.

But God gave him triumph over his brothers, raised his name very high, made him a father of a Pharaoh, the second man in the kingdom and offered him two of the twelve tribes of Egypt.

It is God who says *"For the oppression of the poor for the sighing of the needy, Now I will arise. I will set him in the safety for which he yearns."* (Psalm 11).

If you are poor in spirit God will support you and stand beside you; but if you are a tyrant who thrashes people soundly and treats them unjustly without fear, God will stand against you and give blessings to the poor.

God was with poor Lazarus and not with the rich man. This is why it was said that when Lazarus died, the angels carried him to Abraham's side. The rich man also died and was buried.

In hell he suffered agony, while Lazarus was comforted. (Luke 16:22 - 25).

David also was poor, owing to the tyranny of his son Absalom who betrayed him.

Absalom assembled the people about him, then waged war on his father; but in the end, with God's help, David achieved victory after he had fled, barefoot, from the face of Absalom and had been reproached by Shemei, son of Gera.

Also, **David was poor in regard to Joab, the commander of the army!**

God stood beside the prodigal son who returned to his father's house *saying "I am no longer worthy to be called your son. "* At the same time his elder brother arrogantly refused to enter the house and share the feast with his brother. He also dealt insolently with his father.

Such a deed was not reasonable. The Holy Bible does not mention anything about his return to his father's house.

God helped the poor tax collector and paid no attention to the proud Pharisee.

The Bible said that the tax collector returned home justified, unlike the Pharisee, who had despised him. He said "*God! I thank you that I am not like other men - extortions, unjust, adulterers - or even as this tax collector.*" (Luke 18:11,14).

God was with the thief who was hung on the right-hand side of Jesus' cross. While on the cross, this man said "*We are punished justly*" (Luke 23:4 1).

But the other thief, who forgot his sins and continued to insult the Lord Jesus Christ, perished.

God was also with the poor Canaanite Woman who, with a broken heart, said "... *yet even the little dogs eat the crumbs which fall from their master's table* "(Matt 15:27).

In this woman's humiliation, the Lord perceived faith not found in all Israel.

Surely, The Lord came for the sake of the poor. He said:

"The Spirit of the Lord God is upon Me, because the Lord has anointed Me to preach good tidings to the poor, He has sent Me to heal the broken hearted, to proclaim liberty to the captives and opening the prison to those who are bound." (Is 61:1).

The Lord Jesus Christ came for the sake of these poor people. He did not come for the haughty, nor for those who are puffed up with pride, nor for the sake of those who consider themselves righteous and compare themselves to others...

This is why we should be modest and poor in spirit because God is very close to the broken hearted ones. Give service to all people.

Once, the devil wanted to fight with one of the saints attempting to entice him to vain glory. He said to the saint: "Who are the sheep and who are the goats?"

The Saint said "I only know that I am one of the goats. God knows His sheep."

The devil could not bear the saint's modesty, and went away defeated.

The Measures of Poverty:

Before Christianity, people had different standards with which they would measure anything.

With these standards, no one could consider a poor man a great one.

But Christianity came and changed such measures. The Lord Jesus Christ Himself stood and said "*Blessed are the poor in spirit.*"

It is very clear that poverty of spirit differs from that of the body.

There may be a man who has a weak body, is poor, sick, tired and in spite of this qualitative analysis and his exhausted body, is proud, bad-tempered and puffed up with haughtiness.

But the poor in spirit has a poor soul. It means that he is modest and repentant.

His soul seems to be in dust and ashes however high his post is. He does not elevate himself above others. He does not look at himself as a distinguished person. He does not ask people to revere or magnify him because of his high rank.

Abraham, the father of fathers. He was the greatest man of his time. In the war waged with Kedorlaomer, he defeated the four kings allied against him and rehabilitated Sodom's captivity. Then, the king of Sodom and Melchizedek, king of Salem came out to meet him. (Gen 14:17,18).

In spite of these events, Abraham, bowed down before them when he bought the cave of Machpelah from the Hittites to bury his wife Sarah. (Gen 23:12). They would address him saying *"You are a mighty prince among us."* (Gen 23:6).

Also, when the three men visited him, he hurried to meet them and bowed down to the ground, although he did not know their divine personalities. (Gen 18:2) At that time he was hundred years old. He talked to his visitors with great courtesy *"My Lord, - do not pass on by Your servant."*

Indeed, he is modest, poor in spirit, and his spirit never rises up whatever his post may be...

David, the king and prophet, says *"I am poor and needy."* (Ps 70:5).

The crown, the throne, the leadership of the army, the bowing of the people before him; all these temptations never changed his heart towards God. He used to weep before Him and say *"Have mercy on me, Lord, for I am weak."* (Ps 6:2).

In regard to the phrase "poor in spirit" our Lord Jesus Christ wishes for the spirit to be modest and not proud. In this way the body will follow and the two will be the same.

If the spirit is puffed up with pride and vanity, the body will become like it, but if it aspires to loftiness, the body will do the same.

Pride envelops the features of the arrogant person. Haughtiness is obvious in his looks, his shape, his movements, his manner of sitting and walking. It is also clear in his speech as well as his silence.

All these qualities are signs of self-admiration and paranoia. And the saying goes: "His nose is in the air."

Undoubtedly, pride of the spirit leads to the body's pride.

To the contrary, the features of the poor in spirit are gentle. They are humble in heart.

His looks are dejected, his walk is light, his manner of sitting shows his politeness, his words are sweet. Meekness and peace flow into his voice as it is said in "The Paradise of the Fathers " [Soft voice and light walk.].

Every poverty in spirit must be accompanied by poverty in body. But not every poverty in body proves its owner is poor in spirit.

What are the qualities of the person who is poor in spirit and is worthy of Jesus' blessedness?

He is a person crushed within himself, contrite before God, broken hearted before the people, he is even pounded before the devil!

Poor Within Himself:

The person who is poor within himself is not aggressive. He is not conceited. He perceives himself good for nothing. He considers himself weak and sinful.

Even if people have a good opinion of him, he will not believe them because, from within, he knows himself well.

His deficiencies are obvious and clear before his eyes.

If he hears any word of praise he feels, within himself, that he is unworthy of it. He thinks that the people are deluded in him.

Perhaps, in their eyes, he may look like the white washed tombs which look beautiful on the outside (Matt 23). Merely a sight from outside!!

We do not say that a person is poor because of some humble words he says.

Such words are numerous. Man utters these words but they do not show the true condition of his heart.

Perhaps someone may say to you "I am filled with sin.", but if you blame him for anything or show him that he is wrong, he may not endure it and become agitated.

Without a doubt, such a man is not poor in spirit, whatever indigence he may pretend by his humble words!

But the person who is poor in spirit speaks the words of humility from his innermost soul.

Content with their authenticity, he means them sincerely. He does not utter them with contemptible flattery or pretence.

He says he is weak, a sinner and unworthy. In all these qualities he is truthful with himself. His heart is as pure as his tongue.

If others address him with such words he will not become annoyed. He will say to himself what Saint Moses the Black said to himself when he was cast out:

"They have done good with you, O' black skinned and grey coloured one. As long as you are not a human being, then, why do you stand among the people!?"

It is suitable for you to be poor in spirit, because you have fallen many times. You are also. likely to fall in future because of your weakness. The devil was even able to defeat you through the sins which overcame you, those sins which you struggled with for many years.

Even if the poor in spirit does not fall, he will feel humility. He says to himself: "Perhaps the devils did not wage war against me because they were not aware of my existence or because they despise my religious struggle and consider my efforts unworthy of their labour. There was a young monk who complained to Saint Bishoy of the great wars waged against him by devils. The devils then protested and said, "Who is that young man? We had not yet heard that he had taken his vows; otherwise we could have declared war against him!!"

The poor in spirit says to himself **"I would consider myself proud if I thought that devils declared war against me!. My failures are due to my weakness and not because of devils."**

This person resembles the pupil who fails an examination. Pride never approaches him. He is broken in spirit because of his failure.

If anyone tells him that he is intelligent and clever he will not believe them...

So whenever you remember your sins, be like that man.

Even if you do not fall, keep your spirit poor lest you should slip and err.

The Holy Bible says *"Pride goes before destruction, a haughty spirit before a fall"* (Prov 16:18).

The grace of God may abandon man because of pride. Then he becomes weak before the devil and falls, until he recognises his weakness and never becomes proud.

It is better then for man to know and feel his weakness in order that he may not fall.

Poverty in spirit protects man from falling. He who is poor in spirit does not depend at all on his own strength. He always asks for God's assistance in order to rely on in his weakness...

Very rapidly, help comes to him according to the Psalm that says *"The Lord is near to those who have a broken hearted and saves such as have a contrite spirit."* (Ps 34:18).

The grace of God continually helps these people due to their humility. This is why they are saved from many struggles.

He who is poor in spirit shows his inner humility through his dealings with others.

Poor Before The People:

As the poor in spirit feels weakness within himself and perceives his sins, he respects himself and treats others in the same way.

He cannot show himself high and lofty in comparison to others. He says to himself "Who am I to put myself above others while they are far better than me?!   I who have committed such and such..." This is why, he treats all people with all respect, reverence and respect even if they are younger in age or lower in rank.

He always chooses the least important place. He does so not only to carry out the commandment, but mostly because of his contentment with such things.

If he enters a church he will think himself out of harmony with the sweet tunes. He will also see himself as a spot which spoils the image of the congregation of believers.

This is why speak to anyone as if he has authority. He does not discuss any matter with a responsible person. Generally - in his life - he places himself last and makes himself servant to all.

As the Spiritual Sheikh said "Wherever you are, be the youngest among your brothers and serve them."

The poor in spirit rebukes no-one. Neither does he become angry with anyone or sadden anyone. He asks everyone to bless him and pray for him.

He criticises no-one, judges no-one. He does not defame anyone or mock them. He continually puts the words of God before him "*He who is without sin among you, let him throw a stone at her first.*" (John 8:7).

When he is broken hearted, he never takes it upon himself to be master of anyone.

On the contrary, we find that a young man, who was appointed a Sunday School teacher in the church and had the chance to read the Holy Bible and teach the children well, boldly took it upon himself to be master and guide to all the members of his family group, and supervisor over their work and disciplinarian of all.

Even in his dealings with his parents, he may rebuke and reprimand them, without any respect or courtesy, because of some of their actions.

With haughtiness and maybe even with offence, he draws their attention to God's commandments as if his acquaintance with God led him to haughtiness instead of calling him to humility.

If you blame him politely he will say that he is defending the truth! Then you will be astonished and ask: 'Why does the defence of the truth lack humility? and why does it cause dissatisfaction?'

Undoubtedly, the one who is poor in spirit can defend truth, does so in humility, and first of all, he obtains God's right from himself before claiming such rights from other people.

He follows the advice he gives to others in his own life...

Perhaps he may defend truth through his own life which in itself can be a testimony to the truth.

This is why his life becomes a reprimand to others without rebuking them with his tongue. He remains poor in spirit. His efficient, silent example reproves others for their wrong deeds.

He who knows truth and loves it must understand quite well that he has no right to insult others with the justification of giving testimony in favour of it.

He who is crushed in spirit prefers to be a disciple and not a teacher.

When sitting in an assembly, he will be the last one to speak with the words of the Holy Bible in his mind "*Everyone should be quick to listen, slow to speak*" (James 1:19).

He does not do so because of the virtue of silence, but owing to his true heartfelt desire to benefit from what is said during the discussion.

If they ask him for his opinion, he will say "You are blessed; I like to listen and benefit from what I hear."

Of course, the one whose temperament is like this will not interrupt others when they speak.

He who causes others to be silent in order that he may speak looks down upon them. He feels that what he says is the most accurate and best speech.

This kind of person makes himself administrator over people's discussions.. He says "This is wrong and that is right." In this way he loses his heart's humility and his chaste tongue as well. What is needed is humility of heart and purity of tongue.

Some wrongdoers may apologise only with their tongues and not from their hearts.

The wrongdoer may say "I am sorry for my wrong deed" but the displeased one may not accept his apology because he utters his words without mindfulness, without the required strength, without humility and without any heartfelt emotion. Certainly the injured one is not satisfied.

The wrongdoer may bow low before him but he is rejected. He bows low with his body and not with his spirit.

Mere formalities are false pretence without spirit. They are not accepted. Notice the chanter sings in the Psalm *"I am laid low in the dust myself and not my body"* (Psalm 119). The one whose spirit is laid low in the dust is the one who worships the Father in spirit and truth   (John 4:23).

Such a man prefers all people to himself in humility.

I say in humility because there are some people who stubbornly insist on sitting in a back seat, and defeat others with their opinion.   Some arguments take place after which others are compelled to obey them. This is why, with triumph, they sit in the back seats...

Such stubbornness and persistence have nothing to do with poverty in spirit.

The last place means the last in rank and not in place.

If you consider yourself the last in rank you will be the obedient one who yields and not the head-strong person who subjugates others and goes ahead of them to win the seat.

It is your duty to bring the others forward in prestige and consideration.

You should ask them once and twice to do so, but if they insist on staying where they are, you yourself give way as long as there is nothing in this behaviour against the law or commandments.

For example: If anyone offers you a cigarette and you refuse, your persistence will not be obstinacy against poverty in spirit.

You can refuse in a polite way and say to him. "Pardon me, but I am a weak person, I do not have a strong will If I smoke once, smoking will become a habit I will not be able to get rid of.

Besides, neither my health nor my income can support my smoking. It is safer and better for me to be away from that bad habit. Even the smell of cigarette smoke annoys me". In this way, you can apologise, refuse and resist, but with politeness and humility.

You can also say "I have heard about the disadvantages of smoking, which concern me." If they say to you "Don't worry.", tell them that you are fearful of smoking. Ask them to pray for you in order to remain fearful of smoking.

Here, persistence does not clash with humility and poverty in spirit. The same words are applied to any other similar sin. To insist on resisting sin and temptation is not considered stubbornness.

Poverty in spirit does not mean submission to any kind of sin. The virtue of being poor in spirit is meant to be connected with holiness and purity.

It is wrong to practise one virtue in isolation or in contradiction of other virtues. Virtues complement one another without contradiction.

When dealing with people, the person who is poor in spirit does not defend himself against any blame focused upon him. He does not want to absolve himself because he is sinful.

He also does not wish to exonerate himself before people. His conscience does not allow him to give a different image of himself from the real one.

This is why he listens to them and holds his tongue. He will say within himself "Do they say that I am a sinner? I am indeed a sinner, and even if I am not committing this particular sin, I may be entangled in another one. There is no great difference between the two cases because the result of the two is sin."

Sometimes he defends himself, thinking that doing so may calm others.

For example one person may be angry with another because of certain behaviour, and if the first becomes convinced of the other's wrongdoing, his anger will increase. Perhaps he may lose his love for him. This is why he explains everything, not to justify himself but to soothe his anger in order not to lose the feeling of love he has for the other person. This matter does not clash with poverty in spirit.

A person poor in spirit also does not tell others about his experiences, especially those which elevate him before others.

His relationship with God is supposed to be one of his personal secrets. The Lord mentioned the importance of hiding virtues in Matthew 6.

Although some miracles, which had never been witnessed by anyone on earth, were witnessed and experienced by the Virgin Saint Mary, she did not speak of them. She was a treasure of secrets and a treasure of experience yet *"She kept all these things in her heart."* (Luke 2: 51).

The poor in spirit does not make a comparison which elevates him above other people.

As was said in the "Orchard", if he speaks about others, he will say "This person is more righteous than I." "That man is more learned than I" "This one is better than I in everything" "This person is more cautious and more accurate than me."

Whatever wrong people do, he deals with them kindly. He knows the wrong deeds he had done before. He has experienced how violent the wars of the enemy are. Before people and within himself, the person who is poor in spirit is also:

Poor In The Presence Of God:

This poor person feels unworthy of standing before God. This feeling is manifested through his humble words which resemble the prayer of the tax collector. He shows no pride in his prayer as the Pharisee did. He says the whole prayer with a broken heart.

For example, he says "O, my Lord! Who am I to stand before You and talk with You? You, before whom the angels and archangels stand!! O' Lord, You are modest to listen to a sinner like me who is made of dust!!"

The poor in spirit does not stand before God as a contestant.

He is not like the person, who, in his prayer, claims his rights as a son and heir to the Lord Jesus Christ!!

The one who is broken-hearted says, "I, who am full of sin, and everyday commit sins which make me subject to final judgement, have no privileges at all!!"

What attributes does he have to be a son of God, while the apostle says " *whoever has been born of God does not sin ... but he keeps himself and the wicked one does not touch him*" (1 John 3:9, 5:18).

Do you think that the one who is poor in spirit has a strong heart and dares ask for supernatural gifts!? or misunderstands the phrase *"But earnestly desire the best gifts"* (1 Cor 12:31).

I wonder!! Can the broken hearted one see himself as a worker of miracles, marvels, wonders and signs? Can he speak in tongues? Can he make people see him as a gifted saint?

Gifts are for a person who can bear them, but such a person does not ask for gifts. If he is gifted without asking, the gifts will be given to him accompanied by the humility to endure them.

But he who asks for gifts will easily fall in vain glory because before he asks, he imagines himself worthy of them. This is why we must be wary of this serious matter...

Here, we also say that the word "claim" is far more difficult than the word "ask".

The one who asks is poor. He begs of one who is richer than himself. But the one who claims his rights is a person who owns real property.

He exercises his rights without seeking the favourable inclination of the man who will give them back to him.

The word "*claim* " cannot be applied to the relation between man (the debtor) and God (the creditor), who claims his debt, or with leniency and love forgets all his debts because that debtor has no money to pay him back (Luke 7:42).

The poor in spirit does not pretend to have been reborn, nor that he will do no wrong in future.

We sin every day, and "*If we say that we have no sin, we deceive ourselves and the truth is not in us.*" (1 John 1:8).

If you are saved, renewed, justified and sanctified and do no wrong, then, how can you stand in the presence of God and say in your prayer *"Forgive our debts as we also have forgiven our debtors."* (Matt 6:12)?

With a broken spirit, you can say to the Lord "I cannot forget your favour and kindness forever".

Indeed, my Lord, you cleanse me with hyssop, and I shall be clean; but in spite of that, I return, once more, to corrupt myself."

As the one who is poor in spirit is poor within himself, poor before God and poor before people, he is also:

Poor Before Devils:

When you are proud, you cannot defeat the devils who themselves fell because of own arrogance. You can conquer them with humility. It was in this way that the saints overcame devils.

Take for example Abba Antonios, who said to them when they gathered around him "What do you, who are so strong, want from a weak person like me?" and added "I am weak, too weak to fight the youngest among you." Then the saint cried for help and said "O' Lord, save me from the hands of these devils who think that I am worthy." As soon as they heard his humble prayer, they vanished like smoke.

Once upon a time, Abba Antonios said "I saw the traps of the devils spread over the whole earth, then I cried to God 'O' Lord, who can escape from these traps?" A voice came to him from heaven saying "The humble can escape from them."

This poverty in spirit, which overcomes devils, is quite clear in the words of Saint Macarius the Great.

Once the devil appeared before Abba Antonios and said "What deed can you do that we cannot do? You fast and we abstain from food! You spend the night awake and we do not sleep; you live in the desert and in the wilderness and we do the same thing but with one thing you overcome us."

When Saint Macarius asked him what that thing was, the devil said "You overcome us with your humility."

Blessed are the poor in spirit,

For Theirs Is The Kingdom Of Heaven:

The words of the Lord about poverty in spirit or poverty alone may not satisfy people or persuade them to carry out such instructions. This is why He put before them what would encourage them to carry out His words, I mean the eternal reward, the kingdom of heaven.

"Blessed are the poor in spirit for theirs is the kingdom of heaven" **(Matt 5:3).**

Here, the Lord Jesus Christ raises the thoughts of His congregation from earth to heaven; from paying attention to earthly supremacy to paying attention to the heavenly kingdom and what characteristics it requires, in order that their virtues may shine and be worthy of such a glorious reward.

Here, **the Lord carries people's thoughts from the material world to the kingdom of heaven.**

It is better for them to live here poor in spirit in order that they may live in the heavenly kingdom forever, after the manner of Lazarus, the beggar. (Luke 16).

The Lord also said to them *"Do not lay up for yourselves treasures on earth ... But lay up for yourselves treasures in heaven "* (Matt 6:19,20).

He also said to them *"Do not labour for food which perishes, but for the food which endures to everlasting life"* (John 6:27).

As for their reward, the Lord Jesus carried them to heaven: *"Don't do the good in front of people to be seen by them as hypocrites do. I say to you, they have their reward."* (Matt 6:5).

Do your good in secret, and your Father in heaven who sees you will reward you there publicly.

On earth be poor in your spirits and be confident of receiving your reward. Which reward? It is *"The heavenly Kingdom."*

As for your dwelling place, be strangers on earth and you will reside in heaven.

"The Son of Man has nowhere to lay his head." (Luke 9:58) but He is going to heaven to prepare a place for you. He says *"In my Father's house are many rooms"* (John 14:2).

This is why it was said that the saints would state that they were aliens and strangers on earth; and were longing for a better country - a heavenly one (Heb 11: 13,16). Here, we have no everlasting city.

The Lord Jesus Christ does not want your ambition to be for earthly things but for heavenly ones.

This is why it was said *"Do not love the world or the things in the world because the world is passing away and the lust of it."* (1 John 2:15,17).

This is why the Lord Jesus Christ began to direct people's sights towards the heavenly kingdom from the beginning of the sermon on the mount, as if He wanted to tell to them that He had not come to establish a kingdom for them on earth, as was thought by their leaders.

He came to say *"My kingdom is not of this world"* (John 18:36) and to let His disciples teach that *"Friendship with the world is enmity with God."* (James 4:4), and *"If anyone loves the world, the love of the Father is not in him."* (1 John 2: 15).

During the sermon on the mount, the words "Kingdom of heaven", "heaven" and "the heavenly Father" were

repeated many times. This is the declaration of a new world, a new kingdom and a new, high and prominent standard.

Why? *"For where your treasure is, there your heart will be also."* (Matt 6:21).

He said these words during His sermon on the mount. He wishes people's hearts to be in heaven, high above earthly things, whether these are desires, glories or hopes.

In this way, they can endure being poor in spirit and bear the cross as well.

The person who has their hopes attached to earth, and the one who searches for dignity cannot bear up the cross.

This is why we find that the whole of the sermon on the mount takes the same trend. The one who turns the other cheek, he who goes two miles with the person who forces him to go one mile, the person who will give his cloak if someone wants to take his tunic, he who spends and gives anyone who asks him.

For this reason, all the lessons given in the sermon on the mount about endurance and forgiveness were practical preparations for carrying the cross and for people to accept the idea of the cross as well.

Why? These matters will undoubtedly lead to the heavenly kingdom.

What about dignity? Your dignity is kept for you in heaven. Your dignity lies in your endurance and in carrying the cross, because in this way, you resemble your Lord and look like the prophets who came before you.

This is why He spoke to them about the heavenly kingdom and said, *"Blessed are you when people revile and persecute you, and say all kinds of evil against you falsely for My sake."*

O' Lord! Why do You teach such beatitudes? He gives the answer: *"Rejoice and be glad for great is your reward in heaven."* (Matt 5: 12).

Indeed, no one can understand the sermon on the mount and all instructions of Christianity except in light of *"The kingdom of heaven."*

In the past, the people had no idea about the kingdom of heaven. Their teachers did not tell them anything about that kingdom because they were fully occupied with establishing a kingdom on earth, the kingdom of our father David (Mark 11:10).

The same thoughts were in the minds of those who were busy with the world's affairs and riches. Even the poor were worried about what they would eat or drink, or what they would wear.(Matt 6:25).

No one thought of this kingdom, this is why it was likened to a hidden treasure.

In the Gospel of our teacher Matthew ,in Chapter 13, the phrase "*The kingdom of heaven*" was said many times by the Lord Jesus Christ. "*The kingdom of heaven is like treasure hidden in a field, when a man found and hid, ...*" (Matt 13:44).

What did the man do? "*and for joy over it he goes out and sells all that he has and buys that field.*"

The Lord said these words to show the people that for the sake of the kingdom of heaven you must sell everything, leave everything, renounce everything - even yourself - and accept death, the death of the cross.

The examples presented about the kingdom of heaven in Matthew 13 are many.

The kingdom of heaven is like a man who sowed good seeds. The kingdom of heaven is like a mustard seed. The kingdom of heaven is like yeast. The kingdom of heaven is like a net that was let down into a lake. It is like every teacher of the law who brings out of his storeroom new treasures as well as old.

There are many examples about "*The kingdom of heaven*" in other chapters.

The important matter is that the Lord Jesus Christ wished them to concentrate their thoughts on the kingdom of heaven.

The sermon on the mount was such an introduction to dialogue about this kingdom that Saint Mark the apostle said of the word of Jesus Christ that *"Jesus came into Galilee preaching the gospel of the kingdom of God."* (Mark 1:14).

And as His mission began with the kingdom, we hear the criminal, hanging on the cross, saying: *"Lord, remember me when You come into Your kingdom."* (Luke 23:42).

For the sake of this kingdom, His disciples left everything and followed him.

Some of them left both nets and fishing; others who were tax collectors left their positions. All of them left their relatives, their families, their houses and their towns. Saint Peter the apostle sums up these occurrences and says to the Lord *"We have left all and followed You!"* (Luke 18:28).

Then the Lord answers *"assuredly, I say to you there is no one who has left house or parents or brothers or wife or children, for the sake of the kingdom of God, shall receive many times more in this present time, and in the age to come everlasting life."* (Luke 18:30).

Here, the Lord speaks of the kingdom of God and the age to come and eternal life, which are considered the most important foundations of Christianity.

✦✦✦

CHAPTER TWO

"Blessed Are Those Who Mourn For They Shall Be Comforted"

The gospel of our teacher St Luke reads: *"Blessed are you who weep now, for you shall laugh."* (Luke 6:21).

Is the Christian life a life of sadness and lamentations? Is joy considered a sin?

No, joy is not a sin. The Holy Bible considers joy a fruit of the Spirit. (Gal 5:22). The Lord Jesus Christ says to His disciples *"But I will see you again and your heart will rejoice, and your joy, no one will take from you."* (John 16:22).

Saint Paul the apostle calls for everlasting joy and says *"Rejoice in the Lord always. Again I will say Rejoice!"* (Phil 4:4).

This is why Christianity calls people to be joyful; to have spiritual joy In God. It also calls them to spiritual consolation from the Counsellor, the Holy Spirit.

There are many examples of spiritual joy; joy may be due to triumph over sin or because of the life of repentance. Heaven also takes part in this joy because *"There will be more joy in heaven over one sinner who repents"* (Luke 15:7).

Every spiritual person rejoices at his victory over sin. He also is very glad when others overcome sin.

Another example of spiritual joy is: **Rejoicing because of the spread of the kingdom of God on earth**, rejoicing owing to the spreading of God's word, the growth of the church and peace everywhere.

One of the examples of holy joy is rejoicing in good and in success.

In this regard, Saint John the beloved, said to Kyria, the chosen lady *"I rejoiced greatly that I have found some of your children walking in the truth."* (2 John 1: 4).

He also said to his dear friend Gaius *"I pray that you may prosper in all things and be in health just as your soul prospers... I have no greater joy than to hear that my children walk in the truth.* (3 John 2,4).

This is the true joy which pours out of the Holy Spirit and runs into the heart, while the world's joy is as false as its consolation.

When the Lord asks us to shed tears during our stay on earth it is for our good, on the condition that our weeping must be sacred and leads to heavenly joy.

This reminds me of the proverb which says *"He who makes you shed tears, weeps for you, but he who makes you laugh, laughs at you."*

It is good for you to be sad on earth for a while, then remain joyful forever in heaven as the apostle said *"For godly sorrow produces repentance to salvation not to be regretted."* (2 Cor 7: 10).

The person who spends his life in pleasures and laughter paying no attention to eternal life and negligent of his sins, will not benefit from these false and temporary joys when he stands in front of the pulpit of the Just God.

This is why we see that a life of shedding tears was the characteristic of the sons of God and not only of those who repented. Weeping was the distinguishing characteristic of great saints.

The Holy Bible and the history of the church gives us many examples of the tears of those saints, some of which we quote.

They believed that shedding tears on earth would save them from eternal tears.

On the final day of judgement, tears lead those who shed them on earth and go to heaven in order to extinguish the flames that will surround them. As for those who do not weep for their earthly sins; tears will be awaiting them where there will be no solicitation, as the Holy Bible says *"There will be weeping and gnashing of teeth"* (Matt 8:12). Of course, God will pay them no attention.

How beautiful are the words said by Saint Macarius the Great, before his death!! He grew old, and when he was ninety years of age, his death was near. The monks gathered around him to see him off. He said many words of consolation to them and ended with "My brothers, let us weep here (on earth) instead of shedding tears there (in heaven) where there will be no solicitation. Then he, as well as the other monks, wept."

One of the greatest men mentioned in the Holy Bible, David the prophet, was famous for shedding tears.

He was a king, a judge, leader of the army, father of a large family and was surrounded by all means of enjoyment. He was a man of great talents, a poet, a musician and a mighty warrior. He committed a sin. He knew the tears of repentance as no one had known before. He says *"All night I make my bed swim, I drench my couch with my tears."* (Psalm 6).

The phrase *"I drench"* refers to the quantity of his heavy tears and the phrase *"all night"* means that he continually wept and proves that he returned everyday from work, as a king of great splendour, to shed tears.

I wonder! Did he weep only during the night? No! Because he says *"My tears have been my food day and night."* (Ps 42:3). He also says, *"I mingled my drink with weeping."* (Ps 102:9).

Some of these tears were shed out of repentance; others because of the kingdom.

He says *"Rivers of water run down from my eyes, because men do not keep Your law."*(Ps 119:136).

The tears of Jeremiah the prophet were of this kind, especially his Lamentations. (Jer 9:1).

The weeping of Ezra is of the same kind (Ezr 10:1). Also Nehemiah (Nehemiah 1). There is also the mourning of the priests in the book of Joel the prophet (Joel 2: 17) and the weeping of Paul for those who live as enemies of the cross of Jesus Christ. (Phil 3:18).

In their silence, the tears of the saints were cries heard by God.

David says to God "*Listen to my tears*". He also says "*The Lord heard my weeping*" and "*The Lord accepts my prayer.*" (Psalm 6).

What a wonder!! Some of these tears lasted a lifetime.

God forgave David who heard his absolution from the mouth of Nathan the prophet.

David did not weep for forgiveness, but wept because he was emotional. How? He wanted to proclaim his repentance and to show his love for God. These tears remained with him all his life. Nothing but death could rescue him from them. This is why when he was close to death, he said "*Return to your rest, O my soul, for the Lord has dealt bountifully with you. For You, have delivered my soul from death, my eyes from tears...*" (Ps 116:7,8).

One famous idealistic person was Saint Arsanius the great.

I am astonished!! Who could find a fault in that saint? Arsanius, the man of silence and tranquility who lived in loneliness. A man whom Patriarch Theophilus would ask for a word of benefit, and to accept a visit from him.

He was a man of prayer and he spent the whole night praying from sunset till sunrise.

Out of his extreme love, he wept till his eyelashes fell out one after the other.

While he was plaiting palm leaves he put a towel on his knees for the tears to fall on. As soon as the name of the Lord was mentioned he wept because of his heart's sensitiveness towards God. He called to his mind his human defects and his late return to God (as he took his vows when he was forty years old), then he wept.

A very short time before his death, Pope Theophilus said of him "O' Arsanius, blessed are you because you wept your whole life for this hour."

Saint Isizoros, the priest of the monks' cells, was one of the people who were known to have wept much.

He was the father of three thousand monks. The devils feared him and could not pass in front of his cell or the neighbouring cells where his pupils lived under the protection of his prayers.

He was a man of vision. He was famous for casting out devils. When he prayed, he wept with such a full voice that his pupil, who lived next door, heard him. Once this neighbour said to him "O, my father! Why do you weep?" He said "Because of my sins." The pupil said "Even you, my father, have sins to weep for?" He said "Believe me, my son, if God revealed my sins, three or four people would not be sufficient to share in my weeping."

Nevertheless, we fill the world with filthiness, while God still squeezes our eyes out, as if pressing on a stone, in order that a single tear may fall, but to no avail.

The saints weep all their lives because of one sin; or shed tears without having committed a sin, but we plunge into sin as easily as we drink water, yet we do not weep!

Our hearts are as insensitive as they would be if we did not love God, whom we exasperate.

Here is another example of sensitivity of weeping because of sin:

Saint Pephnotius, who was one of the disciples of Saint Macarius the Great, and succeeded him as head of Iskitus.

He was a great saint to whom God gave the power of casting out devils. Pope Theophilus would ask him for words of benefit.

One day, this great saint said to his disciples "My sons, when I was a lad, during a walk on the road, I saw a cucumber on the ground. I thought it might have fallen from the porters. I took it and ate it. **Whenever I remember that occurrence I weep.**"

This happened when he was a child. But even when he had grown up and became a monk and a father to thousands of monks of great sanctity, he still said, "whenever I remember that occurrence I weep".

The Lord Jesus Christ himself wept though He committed no sin at all. He wept for the sins of other people, and for the death and destruction caused them by committing such sins.

The Lord Jesus Christ wept at Lazarus' tomb when he heard that the people there and even Martha Lazarus's sister said about man who was made in God's image and in His likeness: that his odour had become bad!! (John 11).

He wept when He saw the results of sin and how it separated man from God and exposed him to His wrath.

There is a moving part in the midnight prayer which comments on the story of the sinner woman who wet the Lord's feet with her tears (Luke 7:38).

This part of the prayer says "My Lord, give me springs flooded with tears as those You had gave the sinner woman in the past."

We ask God for this demand every night, not only on a special occasion or in a certain time which comes soon to an end.

Tears stayed close to the saints all their lives. One of the saints said that the weeping soul which is completely crushed before God is that which God talks with in Song of songs saying *"Turn your eyes away from me, they have overcome me."* (Song 6:5).

Every night, you yourself stand before God with a crushed heart and say "O, my Lord, give me springs flooded with tears to weep for my pride, my obstinacy, my passions and my anger. Give me a spring full of tears to weep for my love of the world, my hatred, my enmity and my love of victory over others.

O my Lord, give me springs filled with tears to weep for the sins uttered by my tongue, the sins committed by my body and sins of thoughts which are without number."

If you examine yourself you will find many reasons which cause you to weep...

Beware of self justification which makes you feel that your life is clear and serene and that you have a good relationship with God which would make you feel that there is no cause for tears.

We need to weep every day over our sins and inadequacies.

Our God says "*Turn to Me with all your heart, with fasting, weeping and mourning.*" (Joel 2:12).

This is true repentance which flows from a heart weighed down with sins.

After Solomon the Wise had examined life and all its pleasures, he said "*It is better to go to the house of mourning than to go to the house of feasting, for that is the end of all men; and the living will take it to heart. Sorrow is better than laughter, for by a sad countenance the hearties made better.*" (Eccl 7:2,3).

If a poor man said these words we might think he practised that kind of life, but the one who said them was a king of great wealth who did not deny himself anything his eyes desired. (Eccl 2:10) In his days, silver was as common as stone (1 Kin 10:27).

There was much gold, and in spite of these riches, he considered weeping far better than these.

Here is a question: What are the things which encourage a person to weep?

Things That Encourage Or Prevent Weeping:

1.   **A sensitive heart and a tender temperament**: The sensitive person weeps because he is easily affected. This is why we find that women are quicker to weep than men.

But if a man weeps his weeping will be stronger and deeper. It is caused by a moving force which shakes his power of resistance...

There are some men who are as strong as stone. They endure everything. It is not easy for such men to weep. If anyone of them weeps it will be a serious thing which makes him weep.

The spiritual, sensitive person feels that sin is the most dangerous transgression which makes him weep, because it separates him from God.

It is difficult for hard-hearted people to weep. Cruelty is not an original quality in human nature because God made man in His image and likeness.

God has a tender temperament. So if you find cruelty or harshness in man's nature, they are considered foreign qualities.

If you wish to obtain the gift of tears, keep away from cruelty and harshness.

Cruelty and tears contradict one another. They never meet. They can unite if water and fire become one element.

So, try to keep away from cruelty and its results.

2.   The deeds which do away with tears are: Judging other people and backbiting them especially if these are carried out cruelly and with extreme measures.

Also, reprimanding people. This will be excessively severe if it takes place in public without consideration for the circumstances of others.

He who convicts other people, thinks of their sins only and not of his own sins.

If you think of your sins, tears will come to your eyes, but if you think of the sins of others in order to convict them, tears will automatically leave your eyes.

If God convicted us as we convict others, no one will be saved.

David the prophet speaks to God saying: "*Do not enter into judgement with Your servant, for in Your sight no one living is righteous.*" (Psalm 142).

Someone may ask saying **"What is your opinion about the members of certain sects who always weep and cry aloud when they pray?**

I tell you that the person who prays with tears weeps before God and does not cry aloud in front of other people. He does not gather people about him to witness his tears.

The spiritual person who weeps in prayer is a broken hearted one. He wishes to be alone with God; to shed both his tears and himself before Him as Hannah, mother of Samuel did when she prayed in her heart and wept in silence. (1 Sam 1:10,13).

The tears which are shed silently and with serene sorrow are considered the hottest tears.

They neither raise their voices nor promote themselves.

Sometimes, during the weeping, the voice is unconsciously raised, as David's was when he heard of his son Absalom (2 Sam 19:4), and as Joseph did when he met his brothers (Gen 45:2).

Some loving people may weep for the sins of others.

He sympathises with them as did Jeremiah the prophet, who wept because of the people's sins, and like Ezra and Nehemiah who wept for Jerusalem's people who committed sins during their captivity.

It was said that Saint John the short used to weep when he saw a person commit a sin. He wept much because of the devil's activity which caused people to fall in sin.

He said "My brother fell today and perhaps I may fall tomorrow. He may fall and repent, and I may fall and not repent."

But when we hear of a fall we unkindly judge the one who has fallen.

If you heard that an escaped lion had killed a person in the next town, would you condemn that person because he could not escape from that lion? *"Your adversary, the devil, walks about like a roaring lion.. "* (1 Peter 5:8).

If you hear that an infectious disease has spread to all parts of a city, will you weep for the inhabitants or condemn them?

Would you say that you do not experience the gift of weeping or you yourself prevent it?

You prevent tears with cruelty, harshness and conviction.

You stop them with argument and contention, with shouting, and with concentrating on others' sins which prevents you from remembering your own sins.

3.   Rage and tenseness prevent tears:

The irritable hot-tempered person is a furious, fiery and indignant one.

Through his agitation and anger, he keeps away from tenderness of the heart, which is inseparable from tears.

If anyone says to you "So and so is hot-tempered. He weeps in his fury."

Perhaps that man weeps because someone else tormented him, as Esau wept after he had lost his birthright and said *"Then, I will kill my brother Jacob."* (Gen 27:38,41).

This is not the spiritual weeping we mean. This is like the example of a girl who cannot get what she wants from her parents cannot convince them otherwise. In the end she goes to her room and weeps.

Rage exterminates the gift of weeping

Man in his heated anger thinks of the sins of others. He does not think of his own sins. He considers himself oppressed, unjustly treated and thinks that he is right.

He may think his dignity has been insulted. All these feelings do not agree with tears. They do not produce them, but exterminate them.

4. Plunging into the life of pleasures, delight and transgression causes the loss of tears.

He who practises the pleasure of sin does not weep because he is dominated by lust.

His experience of delight does not give him any chance for holy sorrow.

The prodigal son felt no sorrow when he used to play with his friends, but when he came to himself again, he felt pounded and crushed.

How can a person who is elevated by pride or busy with worldly glories, be sad?

If he feels, as Solomon, that all things are meaningless and chasing them is like chasing the wind, he will be crushed.

Tears do not correspond with sin but go along with repentance and leaving sin, except in the case of the person who is conquered by himself, and is unable to resist sin. He may commit a crime, then weep and ask for help to escape it, and after that, sins again and weeps until grace comes upon him and saves him.

5.   Pride, arrogance and love of dignity exterminate tears.

A man of sacred grief or the one who is conquered and is a person of spiritual weeping is a crushed and broken hearted person and not a proud one.

The conceited person loves dignity; he is busy with himself and how he can be famous in this world, but the one who thinks of eternity weeps, and in this way all the glories of the world diminish before his eyes.

6. Thinking of tears and rejoicing at them cause their loss.

If a person believes that he is a man of tears he will rejoice and become proud. Pride and tears contradict one another. Rejoicing itself is contrary to tears. He will at least be self-satisfied and in this case he will not need tears.

The saints say "If you rejoice while weeping, don't think of your tears but search for the cause of weeping, then you will return to pounding yourself once more."

If man must conceal his tears even from himself, what can we say about those who like to weep aloud in front of others during their prayers!!? They think that their behaviour is spirituality itself.

Temptations and tribulations bring tears.

God allows tribulations to take place in order for man to be crushed. This is why he realises his weakness and knows that the world is not worthy of anything. He directs himself to God.

Tribulations may compel him to weep but the one who is away from temptations may become hard hearted.

The remembrance of death and visiting tombs bring tears. This is why the saints used to remember death and say with the chanter "*Show me O' Lord, my life's end and the number of my days. Let me know how fleeting my life is.*"

When a person remembers death, pride disappears; his desire for the things of the world vanishes. He repents and prepares himself for eternal life.

Remembrance of repulsive sins bring tears.

This remembrance should be accompanied by repentance and sorrow, by remorse and shame, by experiencing the fall. He says *"O' Lord, give me springs of tears like those You gave to the sinful woman."*

CHAPTER THREE

"Blessed Are The Meek, For They Shall Inherit The Earth"

Who Are The Meek?

The meek is the person who has a calm temper...

The Lord Jesus Christ, who was meek, said to His disciples *"Learn from Me, for I am gentle and lowly in heart."* (Matt 11:29). It was said about him, *"He will not quarrel or cry out,. nor will anyone hear His voice in the streets. A bruised reed He will not break and a smouldering flax He will not quench"* (Matt 12:20). The phrase *"cry out"* gives us a notion about *"The meek"*.

The meek one's voice is neither sharp nor loud.

When he talks with people he does not raise his voice. He does not snub them or become agitated.

The meek person is quiet and good natured. He always wishes to win people's affection *"Love is not rude."* (1 Cor. 13:5).

This is why the meek will inherit the earth. He will calmly acquire people's love on earth and win heaven as well.

Here, I'd like to differentiate between a calm temper and a cold one.

The calm lamblike person is not passionate. He does not stir people up.

The cold tempered person may not become agitated but he easily bothers people ...

When he is asked something, he will give the answer in such a cold manner which may aggravate others.

The meek person is quiet; he brings about serenity in others ...

He is also a good hearted person. He likes to please all people and maintain a good relationship with them. Whatever anyone does to him, he does not get angry. He will not be at ease if he anyone is angry with him. He follows the advice of Saint Antonios the Great who said "Let everyone bless you; invoke a blessing upon you." This is why you will enjoy peace and love will all people ...

The meek is a calm person, both internally and externally.

He is not like some people who seem to be calm, while they are disturbed and agitated within themselves.

They suppress their anger for reasons which may or may not be spiritual. Sometimes they do so through respect for their elders or for fear of the consequences of anger.

The meek person is quite calm. His feelings, sentiments and sensations are in complete tranquillity. He enjoys peacefulness of heart. He does not become agitated or bear a grudge...

On his face, there is a gentle, cheerful smile with which he receives whoever talks or deals with him. People never see him frowning or looking angry.

This is why the person who pretends to be calm while he is agitated within, is not really meek. What we can say is that he is training himself to become meek ...

The meek person does not defend himself . He is not spiteful.

Many a time he gives in to others without sorrow. He does not wish to lose anyone's friendship for the sake of his own rights. To make peace with other people is more important to him than clinging to those rights. If he weighs the two on the scales, the scale of peace with others will undoubtedly prevail.

The meek person does these things automatically without debating with himself.

Although the Holy Bible says " *The Lord will fight for you; and you shall hold your peace."* (Ex 14:14), and the apostle also says, *"Beloved, Do not avenge, yourselves, for it is written: Vengeance is Mine; I will repay' says the Lord"* (Rom 12:19).

The meek does not avenge himself at all and does not ask God to take vengeance for him.

It is enough that God defends him, and in this way he suffers no injury. At the same time he does not like anyone to be harmed because of him or for his sake.

With the meek person, mutual understanding is very easy. He causes no trouble to those who deal with him.

In dealing with others, he does not try to gain anything from them but rather to let them win and profit. This is why he is ready to surrender many things to others without sorrow or distress.

Some people sometimes say that the meek person is a simple person!!

Perhaps you may ask yourself, "What forces me to be simple?"

Believe me, if you are so, God will be with you. He will give you more than you give up.

But if you are difficult with others, God will leave you to experience how useful your obstinacy will be to you. This is why the Holy Bible says "Blessed are the meek."

If you hold a discussion or a conversation with a meek person you will find him simple and unpretentious.

He does not argue or interrupt. In dialogues or discussions he does not try to obtain victory but gives you the chance to speak as you like and say what you want as long as the conversation has nothing to do with creed or faith.

If the conversation includes some matters pertaining to faith, he will give his opinion with serenity and simplicity and without hurting the feelings of the one with whom he argues.

Perhaps he may say to him "What is your opinion?" "Is it not right to say such and such?"

He gives his opinion in the form of a question and leaves that powerful, correct and strong opinion to express itself without severity or pride.

As for general matters, one opinion or another makes no difference to him.

The affairs of this vain world are of no importance to him. He does not care for victory in conversations or discussions. He lets others say what they wish to say. He leaves them to do as they like.

This is why he does not discuss any subject or argue with them about matters which are not connected with the salvation of the soul and its eternity. Indeed, he has nothing to do with material and earthly affairs.

In meetings, he sometimes sits silent. No one feels his presence.

As long as he is not charged with any affair; why does he come into view?

If anyone asks him to speak he may say, "I prefer to listen to others and benefit from what they say.", or he may say, "Mr. So and so is blessed and is better than me."

If he speaks he will praise those who preceded him and he may comment and say "It is according to Mr. X opinion." He is very much a gentleman. When he is silent, people love his calmness and silence; and when he speaks they love the style of his speech.

Someone may ask "Does the meek person's silence mean that he is self-absorbed?"

The answer is no. The self-absorbed person does not know how to deal with members of society. This is why he is self-centred and displeased with anyone and anything around him.

But the meek person will be successful in his dealings with people. He loves them and they love him.

If he keeps silent, this will be due to his humility and love, and not because of self absorption. He wants to give others a chance to speak. He gives preference to others. (Rom 12: 10) He keeps silent in order to benefit from the words of others.

He does not like to take part in conflicts or arguments. He prefers peace and gives satisfaction to all who wish to speak.

The meek does not pressure anyone or use violence.

He does not push hard to win the approval of others in a certain matter against their will. He does not protest or use pressure to fulfil his wish...

He does not seek his own comfort but other people's comfort.

This is why those who are associated with him feel comfortable with his companionship.

Anyone who deals with him would say, "Mr. so and so has a gentle spirit. I feel comfortable with him." If you can behave in such a way, then you will be meek.

The meek person does not insist on his own ideas or opinions prevailing.

However, he does not give up his sound principles, nor does he fight with others to defend them. This matter perhaps requires wisdom mingled with meekness.

This is why Saint James the apostle speaks of meekness and wisdom and says "*Who is wise and understanding among you? Let him show by good conduct , that his works are done in the meekness of wisdom.*" (James 3:13) because there are wise men who may insist on the validity of their opinions jealously and with partiality, while boldly explaining them. Such wise men may cause division and confusion!

The apostle says about these men "Such wisdom does not come down from heaven." That is because it lacks meekness.

This is why, the apostle says "wisdom mingled with meekness" *"But the wisdom that is from above is... first pure then peaceable, gentle, willing to yield, full of mercy and good fruit ... "* (James 3:17).

This is the meek, submissive wisdom with which the apostle concludes his comment saying *"Now the fruit of righteousness is sown in peace by those who make peace."* (James 3:18).

It is strange indeed to find that when some people attain some wisdom, or imagine themselves wise men, they lose the life of meekness and serenity and become severe when they defend their opinion.

They hurt the feelings of anyone who disagrees with them!!

Violence may be an easy shortcut which helps a person to reach his aim quickly, but the meek person cannot use it.

If God grants him the wisdom that comes from heaven he will deliver it to people mildly, gently, quietly and in a good way. If he is contradicted at any time, he does not become angry or agitated.

If they are slow to carry out any task he will be patient with them and give them the chance to do what he requests.

This is why it is said that the meek person's ropes are long. It means that he is a man of tolerance. The one who is not meek wishes a task to be carried out quickly, whatever the result.

But the meek person gives his listener a chance, and gives whoever learns from him the chance to gain knowledge according to their abilities; if not today, perhaps tomorrow or the day after. This is dependant on time, over which we have no control.

Forgiveness is one of the meek person's qualities.

If you do him wrong, he will not repay in kind or behave wrongly toward you. If you insult him, he will not rebuke you. He has a special temperament and certain limits, beyond which he cannot venture.

According to the words of Saint John the Beloved, he cannot infringe his principles or do anything wrong but preserves himself, and the evil one cannot harm him (1 John 5:18) and God's seed remains in him. (1 John 3:9).

The meek does not speak from above or in an authoritative manner.

He always forgets his post, however high or advanced it may be. He deals with his subordinates as if he were one of them.

These employees, with such a meek boss, feel that he is a sincere friend. They consider him their elder brother and feel that he gives his instructions in a quiet way and without insolence. This is why they obey him and carry out his orders out of love and not because they are forced to.

The meek person does not defend himself; other people defend him.

If people attack him, they will oppose them saying "Couldn't you find anyone to attack except that good man?"

Perhaps the aggressor's conscience may not even trouble him because of his gross injustice against a violent person but, even after a while, his mind will trouble him because he behaved in an aggressive manner towards a meek person who could not defend himself.

The meek person is the one who can carry out God's commandment "*Do not resist an evil person.*" (Matt 5: 39).

The people surrounding that meek person may become annoyed by what happens to him, while he himself meets such harms calmly, without losing his peace.

In spite of any harm he undergoes, he does not grumble or make any complaint, but accepts all these matters with patience, leaving everything to God.

The meek person is an obedient person but does not trouble anyone. If anyone draws him to an evil thing he will refuse them and make his apologies. He quietly refuses the demand without rebuking anyone.

If people ask him to go with them to a place which causes him to stumble he will say to them, "Weak people like me are troubled by such places. They may fall into depravity. I am sorry; I cannot go with you." In this manner, he expresses his pure opinion without hurting anyone.

The simple, meek person accepts any matter in good faith.

He puts the words of the Holy Bible before him "*To the pure, all things are pure*" (Tit 1:15).

If anyone says something to him which others would consider to be harmful or a show of contempt, he will accept it in good faith and without resentment.

If anyone tells him that what was said to him is sarcastic, he will pay no attention to them. "*Love thinks no evil.*" (1 Cor. 13:5).

The person who is meek by nature does not attempt to change his kind temperament into an irritable one.

If he tries to make any changes he may not be able to do so, and it may not work in his favour.

Each living being has his own temperament that suits him. The mild temperament is suitable for a pigeon, while the daring, brave temperament suits the lion.

It is unsuitable for the lion to imitate the pigeon in its mildness. It is also not fitting for the pigeon to be as ferocious as the lion.

This reminds me of God's commandment "*A woman must not wear men's clothing, nor a man put on a women's garment.*" (Deut 22:5).

Each of them wears what is suitable for him. As this applies to clothes, so also it applies to one's temperament.

Meekness And Holy Zeal:

Here is an important question about meekness.

Isn't the meek person required to carry out the words of the Psalm *"Zeal for your house consumes me. "* (Ps 69:9)?

Must he be quiet in the presence of heretics and those who devise ways of doing evil and who attack the faith?

✤ The answer is that the meek person can defend the faith with holy zeal and face the heretics and opponents with complete politeness, without insulting anyone or making a mockery of them. He speaks in an objective way. **In this respect I have a high opinion of Saint Dedimus, the blind.**

✤ He used to argue with philosophers and heretics in order to convince them, not conquer them. At his hands, many philosophers adopted Christianity and many heretics gave up their heresies. He used to convince them in meekness without a stinging word, insult or reproof. He is not like those who insult the enemies of religion to such an extent as to cause them to hate religion!

Therefore, let jealousy be prudent, full of love and humility.

Beside the phrase *"Zeal for your house consumes me."* we place *"Let all that you do be done with love."* (1 Cor. 16: 14) and the words of the apostle *"I did not cease to warn everyone night and day with tears."* (Acts 20:31).

Here, in this field, I'd like to give a piece of advice:

The Christian virtues are not separated from each other, but are connected. They are incorporated with each other.

The virtue of "holy zeal", for example, is not separated from or independent of a spiritual life, but is mingled with the virtue of meekness and with that of wisdom. It is also combined with gentleness and love.

In this way we attain a complete spiritual life.

Indeed, virtues do not contradict each other, but complete one another...

This is why the spiritual person can attain the ideal form of perfection.

Blessed are the meek, for they will inherit the earth.

What Kind Of Earth Is This?

1. It is the land of the Living about which the chanter sang in the Psalm and said *"I am still confident of this: I will see the goodness of the Lord in the land of living."* (Ps 27:13), or it is "the new land" which Saint John saw in his Revelation (Rev 21: 1) or it is "the land of the living." in which the saints live.

2. The meek person will inherit the same earth in which we live. In addition to winning the heavenly inheritance, he is loved by all who live on this earth because of his meekness.

This is why it is more agreeable to say:

3. The meek person inherits both this earth and the new one:

It means that he will win both earth and heaven together: both the blessings of those who live on this earth, and the companionship of those who have departed this life and gone to the land of the living...

CHAPTER FOUR

"Blessed Are Those Who Hunger And Thirst For Righteousness"

The Meaning Of 'Those Who Hunger And Thirst For Righteousness':

This phrase describes the person who is eager for righteousness. He wants to be nourished by it, eat it, drink it and grow with it.

It also refers to those who hunger and thirst for God, for His ways and commandments, for virtue in detail and for all spiritual things.

The chanter says to the Lord in his long psalm: *"How sweat are Your words to my taste, sweeter than honey to my mouth."* (Ps 119:103)

The same meaning is repeated in many verses of the Holy Bible. The Lord Himself speaks about this same point, saying that He is the living water, that whoever drinks it will never thirst (John 4:14), and that He is the bread of life (John 6:35).

He also says, rebuking the Israelites: *"They have forsaken me, the fountain of living water and hewn themselves cisterns, broken cisterns that can hold no water."* (Jer 2:13).

Blessed are those who thirst for the spring of living water, that is God Himself. They feel eager for Him, to abide in Him, to enjoy His delightful companionship, and to talk with Him.

David the prophet says in his Psalms: *"O, God You are my God, early I seek You,. my soul thirsts for You."* (Ps 63:1).

He also says *"As the deer pants for the water brooks, so pants my soul for You, O' God. My soul thirsts for God, for the living God."* (Ps 42:1).

This, of course, is holy thirst. The chanter says about food: *"I will lift up my hands in Your name. My soul shall be satisfied as with the marrow and fatness"* (Ps 63:4,5).

This is godly love which fills the soul. Man is made of a body, made of dust and spirit. The body is satisfied with material bread, but the spirit lives on every word that comes from the mouth of God. (Matt 4:4; Deut 8:3).

This is why the spirit becomes hungry and is in great need of the word of God which feeds it.

He who abstains from food and does not feed himself on spiritualities, feels hunger of the body.

But he who is fed with spiritual food does not easily feel bodily hunger.

This is why we do not feel any hunger during the holy Pascha in Passion week .Although our bodily fast is severe and difficult, we do not feel any hunger because we feed ourselves on the mournful tunes which deeply affect the soul, and on the holy readings and rituals of this week.

We feed ourselves on its remembrances, sensations and contemplations.

Our souls become hungry and thirsty and need those holy days with their filling spiritual food.

Our souls are not in need of food; on the contrary, they feel hunger and thirst for fasting.

There is a great difference between hunger and thirst for bread and water to support the body, and hunger and thirst for righteousness in order to feed the soul which is nourished on virtue, contemplations, tunes and readings.

The soul is also fed with the sacrament of Eucharist, so it hungers for it...

About this subject, Our Lord Jesus Christ says "I am the bread of life" "I am the bread that came down from heaven." "*If anyone eats of this bread he will live forever. And the bread that I shall give is My flesh, which I shall give for the life of the world." "Whoever eats My flesh and drinks My blood has eternal life and I will raise him up at the last day." "He who eats My flesh and drinks My blood abides in Me and I in him."* (John 6:33-56).

Blessed is the man who hungers for this holy sacrament and finds nourishment in it.

He likes to take Holy Communion, which sanctifies both his heart and his mind and prepares him spiritually.

It gives him a strong will to abide in God and makes him careful not to fall and live a correct life for the sake of the dignity of this great sacrament.

This is why he hungers for it and is eager to have it and says in his heart, "When can I have that holy flesh and noble blood?"

The Life Of Heavenly Love:

To hunger and thirst for righteousness means that you are longing for God, because there is nothing more righteous than to be in love with God.

About this matter, says the Virgin in the Song of Solomon: " *I charge you O' daughters of Jerusalem, if you find my beloved that you tell him I am lovesick.*" (Song 5:8).

How strong and deep is this love which delights man's heart and senses so tenderly that he becomes sick with love.

If he prays, his prayer will not be compulsory, but a declaration of love which expresses the inner feelings that come from the heart and not from the lips.

This man feels thirsty to talk to God, to quench his thirst with prayers.

Because he is filled with a great desire for God, he says with David, the chanter *"When can I go and meet with God?"* (Ps 82:2).

This man, who has such a strong desire for God, also has the same longing for the house of God. This is why he says along with David the prophet: *"How lovely is Your tabernacle, O' Lord of hosts! My soul longs, yes, even faints for the courts of the Lord"* (Ps 84:1).

Then he does not go to the house of God merely as a habit, or to perform a spiritual duty, but because his soul longs to enter the courts of the Lord.

This is a hunger and thirst for the church. This is why, the prophet, also, says *"I was glad when they said to me, Let us go to the house of the Lord."* (Ps 121:1) *"Blessed are those who dwell in Your house, they will still be praising You."* *"For a day in Your courts is better than a thousand."* (Psalm 83).

Also, David said *"One thing I have desire of the Lord, that I will seek: that I may dwell in the house of the Lord all the days of my life."* (Psalm 27).

Perhaps you may ask "What is this you long for, O' great king, though you have all the luxuries of kings? Why do you feel hungry? Why do you feel thirsty? What attracts you to long for such a life?"

He answers *"To behold the beauty of the Lord and to inquire in His temple."* (Ps 27:4).

This prophet, deep in his love for God, did not only long for the courts of God, His word and to speak to Him, **but he was hungry and thirsty for God himself.**

This is why he says "Your face, Lord, I will seek. Do not hide Your face from me." This is the true spirituality followed by those who love the Lord, who hunger and thirst for Him.

If this is so, what can we say about the persons who do not go to His house unless we try many times to convince them, bring them back, and compel them using many different methods?

What can we say about those who pray or read the Holy Bible by force and do not fast without first conquering the will and subduing the body?

Spiritual people hunger and thirst for God because He is the tree of life.

He is the true vine (John 15:1) and the cluster of life. We thirst to be united to him as the branch is to the vine, the branch into which the vine's sap flows to give it life.

Our food is to do His will (John 4:34). This is why our hearts rejoice at His satisfaction and His heart is pleased with our obedience.

It is understood from the continuance of hunger and thirst for righteousness that a believer cannot reach

spiritual satisfaction, because the search is continuous. The more he lives with God, the more he feels new spiritual enjoyment which ignites him so hotly that he becomes more and more eager to live deeply with the Lord.

This is why he continues to hunger and thirst for more and more spiritual enjoyment which cannot be expressed.

Aren't there many kinds of material foods about which some say: "One cannot become satisfied with eating this kind of food, whatever its quantity may be?" How much more, then, is spiritual food?

Did St. Paul the Apostle feel satisfied with what he attained in his spiritual journey?

Even after being caught up to the third heaven and hearing inexpressible things that man is not permitted to speak of (2 Cor. 12:4), he says " *Brethren, I do not count myself to have apprehended; but one thing I do: Forgetting those things which are behind and reaching forwards to those things which are ahead. I press towards the goal to win the prize of the upward call of God in Christ Jesus.* " (Phil 3:13-14).

This continuous attempt, and this desire to strain towards what lies ahead are undoubtedly hunger and thirst for righteousness.

The true spiritual life is a journey towards perfection which has no limits. This is why it requires continuous effort and perpetual longing for the infinite kingdom.

What we receive on earth is a mere taste of the heavenly kingdom. The taste is never satisfied. It makes man hungry and thirsty and anxious to get much more of what he has tasted.

This does not affect him alone, but he calls the others saying: *"Taste and see that the Lord is good."* (Psalm 33).

Satisfaction with spirituality certainly leads to laziness.

Hunger And Thirst With Respect To Prayers:

Our fathers the saints were not satisfied at all, but used to escape from people to be alone with God; to be detached from the whole and united with the One. The more they enjoyed association with the Lord, the more thirsty they became. In this way, their unity with God, their being alone with Him and their discourse with Him increased.

We have two great examples: Saint Arsanius and Saint Macarius the Alexandrian.

Saint Arsanius was always silent so as not to sever his attachment to God because of his speech with people. He used to spend the whole night standing and praying from sunset to sunrise.

But Saint Macarius, the Alexandrian suppressed his mind and trained it not to keep any other thought except for those concerning God and divine matters.

These are some of the models of love for heaven about which we can say. *"Sweet is Your name and blessed in the mouths of Your saints."*

This is a phrase taken from Saturday's Psalmodia. It might have been taken from David's Psalm 119 which says, *"Beloved is Your name which is my recital all the day."* The saint feels such spiritual delight in God's name that he reiterates it with love.

It is not only a mere law of prayer or a liturgy or a religious rite, but also a sentiment ... hunger and thirst for this name which alleviates the thirst of the heart and all its feelings.

Hunger and thirst in regard to love may sometimes cause tears to be shed...

Hence, weeping during prayers may take place. It is the weeping resulting from love and great longing, which reminds me of the story of Jacob, the father of fathers when he met his son Joseph after longing to see him for decades.

The holy Bible says *"So Joseph made ready to meet his father; and he presented himself to him, and fell on his neck and wept on his neck a good while.* (Gen 46:29).

These are the tears of joy and longing. They express hunger and thirst of feelings in a manner clearer than language and words.

Sometimes, longing of the heart becomes too strong for it to bear, and for this reason man weeps because such longing cannot be borne even by the eyes... It is a hunger and thirst that cannot be quenched or satisfied except by tears.

Perhaps, most of the saints' tears were a result of thirst to depart to God where they could enjoy His companionship for eternity, without hindrance.

Hunger and thirst may express longing and yearning.

The person who prays because of his longing is not like the one who performs it as a duty.

Likewise, the person who fasts because of his longing differs from one who does it as a duty.

Here is an example for each of them:

What feelings would a spiritual person have during the fifty holy days before Pentecost, when there is neither fasting nor prostration, for which he longs, and while the laws of the church prevent him from doing these things? How would he feel, then, when those holy days come to an end and the fast of the holy apostles begins? With what sentiments and longing will he fast and begin his prostrations?...

The one who longs for prayers holds a special memento which is shown to him when he prays. Whenever his prayer comes to an end, he finds himself unable to stop praying. He clings tighter to God.

He refuses to conclude his talk with the Lord. He tries to prolong his prayer by adding phrases and verses to it.

He is like the child who is going to be weaned from his mother's breast. Forcibly, they take him away from the bosom of his mother while he completely refuses to do so as all his longing is for his mother's breast.

The vital force of prayer will remain in the mind and in the heart of this person even if he ends his time of standing up to pray.

Even if he leaves his house and goes onto the road, the words of his prayer will follow him and flow into his mind. They accompany him in his walking and in his sitting down. They permeate his work and offer him sacred silence. Anyone who speaks to him feels as if he is taking him away from his mother's bosom by force. It is as if someone comes and tries to snatch John, the apostle, from Jesus' bosom to have Him do something needed by the brethren.

It is also as if Martha wishes to prevent Mary from sitting at the Lord's feet.

One of the signs of hunger and thirst with respect to prayers is that the person who prays almost has no sense of what is going on around him.

Because he is engaged wholly with God, he senses none of the things around him. It is like the story of Saint John the Short and the camel keeper, who spoke to him many times without John hearing what he had said.

All his senses were concentrated on his prayer and nothing else, as if he and the Lord were alone in the. universe. He looked like a starving person who had found an appetising meal before him.

Sentimental people are nearer to God than others.

When they form a relationship with the Lord, they pour out their feelings, and it becomes an informal relationship, unlike those of whom God said "*These people draw near to Me with their mouth and honour me with their lips, but their heart is far from me*". (Matt 15:8).

To show how important feelings are, we say that the adulterers who turned from sin turned towards God. They very quickly became saints because, through their complete repentance, they presented to God their sentiments which they had previously given over to sin, and became hungry and thirsty for God. **If man's heart is filled with worldly affairs he will never feel hungry or thirsty for God.**

He cannot love both God and the world. Either he loves one or the other, because anyone who chooses to be a friend of the world becomes an enemy of God (James 4:4).

If man is met by a certain sin and loves it, he will have no longing for God, nor will he feel hunger nor thirst for Him.

Repentance therefore precedes hunger and thirst for God, then it accompanies him on the journey. Also, hunger and thirst for to God leads to repentance.

When can we attain all these sentiments?

We, at whose doors God is still knocking, and we have not yet opened to Him.

"Blessed are those who hunger and thirst for righteousness for they will be filled."

They Will Be Filled:

They will be filled with heavenly love; with spiritual enjoyment and with consolation from heaven. They show their longing for God while God longs for them much more. This is why He grants them His love and they in turn feel the pleasure of God's companionship ... things which words cannot express.

But I say that this fullness is a temporary one. It is a mere taste.

"Taste and see." The more God reveals Himself and opens His heart to them the more He gives them, the more hungry and thirsty they become, because man can never be satisfied with God's love.

I wonder if we shall we feel complete satisfaction in eternity? Or will it be a temporary satisfaction which will cause us to be more eager? And will eagerness satisfy us or bring us more thirst?...

In truth, I don't know.. God alone knows.

CHAPTER FIVE

"Blessed Are The Merciful For They Shall Obtain Mercy"

Mercy Is One Of God's Qualities:

Mercy is one of God's qualities and the merciful one bears a His likeness.

It was said about God "*The Lord is merciful and gracious, slow to anger, abounding in mercy. He will not always strive with us, nor will He keep His anger forever. He has not dealt with us according to our sins. Nor punished us according to our iniquities. For as the heavens are high above the earth, so great is His mercy towards those who fear Him; as far as the east is from the west, so far has He removed our transgressions from us.*" (Ps 103:8-12).

God's wonderful mercy was manifested strongly and clearly on the cross.

There He took the sins of all human beings upon His shoulders and forgave them. He is the merciful, good God, who does not take any pleasure in the death of the wicked. Rather, he is pleased when they turn from their ways and live (Ezek 18:23).

He is the God who pronounced the judgement of destruction on the Ninevites, and when they repented and turned from their evil ways He had compassion on them and did not bring upon them the destruction He had threatened (John 3:10).

It is God who sometimes threatens, then becomes overcome by His compassion.

In His mercy, God received the repentant people without insulting them.

In Chapter 15 of the Gospel of Saint Luke the Evangelist, He presented three stories about His acceptance of the repentant, the lost and the straying: The lost sheep, the lost son and the lost coin.

He mentioned how God searched for them and how He rejoiced at their return without rebuking anyone.

The Lord received Simon Peter in the same way after the resurrection. He did not hurt his feelings or mention how Peter had denied Him by saying "*I don't know the man.*", but restored him to his apostolic rank and said to him "*Feed My lambs,. take care of My sheep.*" (John 21).

In His mercy, the Lord had compassion on the scattered people.

About this, the Holy Bible says *"But when he saw the multitudes, He was moved with compassion for them, because they were weary and scattered, like sheep having no shepherd."* (Matt 9.36).

In the midnight absolution found in the Agpeya (prayers of the canonical hours), we pray for the sake of such people saying *"O' God, remember the helpless, the bedridden and those who are not remembered by anyone."*

God is merciful. He helps those who are helpless.

In our prayers we say "O' God, helper of the helpless, hope of the hopeless, consolation of the poor in spirit and harbour to those who struggle in the tempest."

Is there any other mercy we can ascribe to God? The person who takes care of such miserable people follows the example of the Lord.

Because the Lord is merciful, He made mercy superior to adoration. He said: *"For I desire mercy, and not sacrifice."* (Hos 6:6).

In every place and at all times, people knew that God was merciful.

When Nathan the prophet laid three options before David for him to choose from, David said: *"Let us fall in the hands of the Lord, for His mercies are great, but do not let me fall into the hands of men."* (2 Sam 24:14).

How strange this is!?! If we are in the hands of the all Holy, the perfect in His Holiness, in His Goodness and in His Righteousness, He will protect us and will not deal with us according to our sins but will respond to us when we say "According to Your mercy and not to our sins."

But if we fall into the hands of man, he will not sympathise with us, and although he resembles us in our sins and weaknesses, he would insult us at every turn.

The Importance Of Mercy:

Because mercy is so important, God made it a measure for condemnation in the final judgment.

On the last day, God will say to those on His left *"Depart from Me, you cursed, into the everlasting fire prepared for the devil and his angels"* (Matt 25:41).

Why did He give this sentence? He says immediately after this *"For I was hungry and you gave Me no food, I was thirsty and you gave Me no drink, I was a stranger and you did not take Me in, naked and you did not clothe Me, sick and in prison and you did not visit Me.*

Then, he explains the reason saying *"Whatever you did not do for one of the least of these, you did not do for Me."* (Matt 25:42-45).

Therefore, those people perished because they did not show mercy to the needy.

This means that although you have your prayers, contemplations and hymns, if you are not merciful, you will find no mercy on the Last Day when you stand before God who will say "*I desire mercy, not sacrifice.*" (Matt 9:13).

This is why the church teaches us to say in the third service of the midnight prayer:

"In the final judgment, there will be no mercy to those who were not merciful " But, "blessed are the merciful, for they shall obtain mercy." (Matt 5:7).

The Lord uses this measure when He deals with people, whether mercy with respect to worldly material matters such as hunger, thirst and illness, or with dealings, or spiritual affairs.

In all cases He gave a final decision saying "*With the same measure you use, it will be measured to you and to you who hear, more will be given."* (Mark 4:24).

If you deal mercifully with people, God will do the same with you. But if you deal with others cruelly, you will not deserve mercy. Our Lord says "*For with what judgement you judge , you will be judged."* (Matt 7:2).

This is why the Lord advises us saying "*Therefore whatever you want men to do to you , do also to them.*" (Matt 7:12).
If you wish to be treated mercifully, treat others mercifully.

He who is merciful shows the Lord to others and mercy goes before him.

This is why the Holy Bible says *"Blessed is he who considers the poor; the Lord will deliver him in time of trouble"* (Ps 41:1).

On the other hand He says *"Whoever shuts his ears to the cry of the poor, will also cry himself and not be heard."* (Prov 21:13).

Your mercy on others precedes you and intercedes for you before God.

If you show mercy to others, God will be merciful towards you. But if you are harsh and fierce, do not protest if you receive the same treatment. As for forgiveness, the Lord said, *" Condemn not and you shall not be condemned. Forgive and you will be forgiven"* (Luke 6:37).

In the same verse He also said *"Do not judge, and you will not be judged."*

Then He said *"Give and it will be given to you; good measure, pressed down, shaken together and running over, will be put into your bosom. For with the measure that you use, it will be measured back to you"* (Luke 6:38).

Concerning forgiveness, the Lord also said *"For if you forgive men their trespasses, your Heavenly Father will also forgive you. But if you do not forgive men their trespasses, your Father will not forgive your trespasses."* (Matt 6:14,15).

He who does not forgive keeps forgiveness away from himself.

103

Even if he was forgiven in the past, it will be taken away from him.

On this subject, the Lord taught us the parable of the debtor (Matt 18:23-35).

To sum up the parable, there was a servant who owed his master ten thousand talents. His master took pity on him and cancelled the debt.

When the servant went out, he found one of his fellow servants who owed him a hundred denarii. He had no compassion on him, and had the man thrown into prison until he could pay the debt.

When the master found out what had happened, he called the servant in and said, *"You wicked servant," "I forgave you all that debt because you begged me. Should you not also have had compassion on your fellow servant, just as I had pity on you?"*

In anger, his master turned him over to the jailers to be tortured, until he could pay back all he owed.

The Lord concluded saying: *"So My heavenly Father also will do to you. If each of you, from his heart does not forgive his brother his trespasses."* (Matt 18:35).

The Grandeur Of Mercy And Its Signs:

Because of mercy, the Lord preferred the Samaritan, a foreigner, to both the priest and the Levite: Perhaps the priest would excuse himself, saying that he had incense to raise or a sacrifice to offer and had no time to take care of the traveller whom the robbers had wounded and left half dead!

Perhaps the Levite would apologise, saying that he was serving in the house of God.

Neither of their apologies not accepted, because God desires mercy not sacrifice (Matt 12:7).

But the Lord praised the good Samaritan because *"And when he saw him, he had compassion on him; and went to him and bandaged his wounds... and took care of him."* (Luke 10:33-34). He considered him to be the only one worthy of the title of "neighbour" because he showed mercy.

Mercy is connected with people's condemnation of each other.

There are people who judge others harshly and cruelly. This does not show mercy and may perhaps turn into a case of oppression.

Such judgment of others may include insults and biting remarks without any consideration for the circumstances of others.

It strictly concentrates on faults. For example, Job's friends reproached him without mercy till he said to them "*How long will you torment my soul and break me in pieces with words? These ten times you have reproached me.*" (Job 19:1,2). "*I also could speak as you, if you were in my place.*" (Job 16:4). "*Have pity on me, my friends, have pity, for the hand of God has struck me.*" (Job 19:21).

The merciful person forgives and excuses others. He does not treat them with severity.

Instead of being hard in his reproach, he tries to find an excuse for them. Jesus Christ's behaviour was the same. When His disciples slept during the most critical time and could not stay awake for even an hour, He forgave them and said "*The spirit indeed is willing, but the body is weak.* (Matt 26:41).

When He was on the cross, with all empathy, He made a plea for those who crucified Him saying, "*Father, forgive them for they do not know what they do.*" (Luke 23:34).

During the prayer for the departed, the church makes a plea on their behalf, saying "As they lived in this world in flesh ".

And also says "*Because, there is no one who is free from sin, even if he spends only one day on earth.*"

Saint Paul the apostle asked for mercy for the sake of his brothers who did not stand by him when he was arrested. He said "*At my first defence, no one stood with me, but all forsook me. May it not be charged against them.*" (2 Tim 4:16).

106

For these reasons, people love the father confessor who is characterised by mercy.

They love the good hearted confession father who considers view the psychological state of the person who comes to him shyly and apprehensively. He does not rebuke him severely, nor despise his failure. He does not shrink from what he hears him say, nor does he deal with him in a destructive manner, But rather he shows compassion, however great his fall may be. He prays for him and asks God to give him power, repentance and forgiveness, because he is a compassionate father who knows the weakness of human nature and the strength of the devil who fights it...

Saint Moses the Black was treated with the same kindness when he repented.

God prepared a very tolerant confession father, St. Isotheres the priest, for him; this man was compassionate towards sinners. This saint embraced him easily from the beginning and led him peacefully until he became a saint.

One night, Moses the Black came to the saint ten times and the saint did not get worried. He advised him to stay in his cell, but Moses answered that he was not able to because the war was very severe upon him. However, through the patience of his spiritual father, the war was taken away from him and Moses grew in spirit.

A merciful heart has compassion upon sinners, no matter how great their fall may be.

He puts before his eyes the words of St. Paul the Apostle, *"Remember the prisoners as if chained with them, and those who are mistreated, since you yourselves are in the body also"* (Heb 13:3).

In his mercy, the Lord Jesus Christ had compassion upon the woman who was caught in the very act of adultery. He saved her from those who wanted to stone her and said, *"Neither do I condemn you, go and sin no more"* (John 8:11). He also defended another sinful woman who washed His feet with her tears in the house of Simon the Pharisee (Luke 7:44).

A merciful heart also is not spiteful. It does not repay evil for evil, but follows the Lord's commandment *"do good to those who hate you"* (Matt 5:44). If people hate you...do not be like them.. If they treat you harshly, do not do the same. Cruelty and vengeance do not agree with mercy.

Cruelty:

Cruelty goes against mercy and is of two kinds:

Cruelty towards people, and cruelty towards God.

Cruelty towards people is well known. It means treating them violently or harshly, or tormenting them, showing disregard for them, and the like, while cruelty towards God is rejecting Him and refusing to respond to His voice within a person. An example of this is Jerusalem, who rejected the many prophets sent to it by God, and even stoned and killed some of them... It did not listen to God's voice on their tongues... So the divine inspiration says, *"If you hear His voice, do not harden your hearts"* (Heb 3:7).

Perhaps Pharaoh had both kinds of cruelty: He treated the people harshly, and when they begged him to decrease the burden, he imposed more tasks on them. He ordered the taskmasters not to give them straw to make bricks and to let them collect it themselves and make the same quota as before... When the people complained, he said, *"You are idle! Idle!"* (Ex 5:6-17).

Pharaoh was also hard-hearted, as he did not respond to God's voice despite the wonders performed before him by Moses and despite the ten plagues...

The Spirit of God cannot dwell in the heart of a cruel person.

He cannot dwell in an obstinate, spiteful or merciless heart as the Holy Bible says, *"The fruit of the Spirit is love, joy, peace and gentleness"* (Gal 5:22). Violence contradicts all these things. This is why the Spirit of God cannot find a place to rest in a hard, cruel, violent heart.

St. Stephen rebuked the Jews for the cruelty of their hearts. He said to them, *"You stiff-necked and uncircumcised in heart and ears. You always resist the Holy Spirit as your fathers did, so do you. Which of the prophets did your fathers not persecute? And they killed those who foretold the coming of the Just One, of whom you now have become the betrayers and murderers. "* (Acts 7:51-52).

After death, hard-hearted people are tormented by images of their cruel deeds.

All the deeds through which they tormented others follow them, appear before them and cause them trouble. They cannot escape them. They remind them of their merciless hearts...

The image of Abel being murdered by his brother undoubtedly followed and troubled Cain not only in heaven but on earth also... For God said to him, "*The voice of your brother's blood cries out to Me from the ground*" (Gen 4:10).

To Whom Will God Show Mercy?

We said that mercy is one of the qualities of God. Who, then, will be worthy of His mercy?

1.   **God shows mercy to those who ask for it with all their hearts.**

This is why, we daily and continually ask God to have mercy on us.

In the introductory prayer of each hour, we recite psalm 51 which begins with the phrase "Have mercy on me, O God, according to Your lovingkindness." and we conclude every hour with the prayer "Have mercy upon us O' God, have mercy upon us." When we enter the church and bow down towards the holy temple, we say "*But as for me, I will*

110

come into Your house in the multitude of Your mercy, in fear of You I will worship towards Your holy temple" (Ps 5:7).

During the raising of incense in the evening and the morning, the priest recites the hymn "Ephnouti Nai Nan" which means "O' God, have mercy on us."

He begins each hourly prayer with the phrase "Ep-shoi-d nai nan" which means: "O' God, have mercy on us."

These prayers might have been quoted from the prayer of the tax-collector who said *"God be merciful to me, a sinner."* (Luke 18:13).

During each prayer we say "Kyrieleison" forty one times which means "O' God, have mercy on us." Does each person who asks for mercy get it according to the promise of God *"Ask and it will be given to you; seek and you will find"* (Matt 7:7)? Or is this conditional? Yes, it is:

2.   God has mercy on those who show mercy to others.

This is why He said *"Blessed are the merciful for shall obtain mercy."* (Matt 5:7).

So we say in the midnight prayer "He who is not merciful will receive no mercy on the Last Day."

The cruel people who have no mercy on others are unworthy of God's mercy. They may remember their lack of kindness when they are in need of mercy and are unable to find it.

When Joseph's brothers experienced hardship in Egypt, they said to one another "Surely we are being punished because of our brother. We saw how distressed he was when he pleaded with us for his life, but we would not listen; that's why this distress has come upon us." *But Reuben answered "Did I not speak to you saying 'Do not sin against the boy?' and you wouldn't listen? Therefore behold, this blood is now required of us."* (Gen 42:21-22).

And when the charge was trumped up against them, and Joseph's cup was found in Benjamin's sack, Judah threw himself to the ground before Joseph and said to him *"How shall we clear ourselves? God has found out the iniquity of your servants."* (Gen 44:16).

3.   To the contrary of that: God will show mercy to the oppressed, even if. they do not ask Him to do so.

The mere iniquity under which they live shouts to God, asking for His justice.

This is why the Lord said, "*I have surely seen the oppression of My people ... I have heard their cry because of their t taskmasters, for I know their sorrows. So, I have come down to deliver them out of the hand of the Egyptians."* (Ex 3:7,8).

He also said in the psalm; "*For the oppression of the poor, for the sighing of the needy, Now I will arise. I will set him in the safety for which he yearns."* (Psalm 11).

Divine Inspiration also says "*Who executes justice for the oppressed. The Lord gives freedom to the prisoners. The Lord opens the eyes of the blind. The Lord raises those who are bowed down. The Lord watches over the strangers . He relieves the fatherless and the widow*" (Psalm 145).

The Lord reclaims the rights of the oppressed from their oppressors.

When **Saint Macarius the Great** was a youth, it happened that a girl conceived through having committed adultery. After the secret had been revealed, the adulterer suggested that she accuse Macarius, who lived in seclusion (before he went to Eskete). So people came to him, insulted him severely and charged him with the expenses of both the girl and her illegitimate child after the birth.

Then, the Lord interfered. It was a difficult delivery. As the pains were unbearable, the girl could not find any way to save herself except to confess that she had wrongly accused that righteous man.

Naboth the Jezreelite was greatly oppressed by Ahab and Jezebel.

God avenged Naboth's blood. He said to Ahab through Elijah ". This is why the Lord said,. *"In the place where dogs licked up the blood of Naboth , dogs shall lick up your blood* !" (1 Kin. 21:19).

The Lord showed mercy upon Mordecai also; He took revenge on Haman who had treated Mordecai unjustly.

Haman had planned a conspiracy against Mordecai. He made a gallows fifty cubits high on which to hang him.

Meanwhile, the Lord interfered and spoke to the heart of king Xerxes and revealed to himMordecai's past glorious deeds, and the evil ones of Haman. Then the king said to his attendants *"Hang Haman on the gallows he had prepared for Mordecai"* (Est 7:9-10).

The Lord also showed mercy to Moses and his people and saved them from Pharaoh's cruelty.

Therefore, Moses and his people were rescued from Pharaoh's slavery when the Lord swept his chariots and horsemen into the Red Sea.

The Lord supported Moses against Aaron and Miriam when they spoke against him.

The Lord defended Moses and made him a man of authority before them, He rebuked them and struck Miriam with leprosy and did not forgive her in spite of Moses' advocacy for her. So Miriam was confined outside the camp for seven days (Num 12:9-15).

On the other hand, God did not support Moses when he killed the Egyptian and hid him in the sand. (Ex 2:14).

There are many other examples which show how the Lord stands against oppressors.

The Lord supported young David against king Saul when this king treated him unjustly and wished to kill him. Saul's end came and the Spirit of the Lord departed from him (1 Sam 16:14).

At last David conquered but when he wanted to deal harshly with Nabal, God sent Abigail to rebuke him (1 Samuel 25). .

The Lord was also against Cain when he killed his brother Abel. God punished him and he became a fugitive and vagabond on earth (Genesis 4).

The Lord shows his mercy to all people, but He does not have compassion upon the oppressors because the measure they use will be measured to them (Matt 7:2).

Perhaps the punishment they receive is powerful enough to turn them from the cruelty in their hearts and from treating others unjustly. But if they resist, they would become an example to others. For this reason, be oppressed througout your life and not an oppressor; be crucified and not a crucifier.

4.   God shows mercy to the weak, the banished, the rejected and the crushed.

The Lord supported the broken hearted tax-collector who went home justified before God. Contrary to this was the proud Pharisee who convicted others. (Luke 18:14).

The Lord supported Zacchaeus, who climbed a sycamore - fig tree to see him, paying no attention to those who considered him a sinner. (Luke 19:6,7).

The Lord showed mercy to the sinful despised woman who was caught in the very act of adultery and rebuked those hard hearted people who wished to stone her saying "*He who is without sin, among you, let him throw a stone at her first.*" (John 8: 7).

5.   God shows mercy to the person who has no one to treat him with compassion.

He did so with the invalid of Bethesda who had been sick for thirty eight years and had no one to help him into the pool. (John 5:7).

This is why, when we pray, we say that the Lord is the helper of the helpless, and the hope of the hopeless. So the Lord showed mercy upon Lot when the people of Sodom moved forward to break down the door of his house. (Gen 19).

Our merciful God moves gradually according to our capacity. He will not let us be tempted beyond what we can bear. But when we are tempted, he will also provide a way out. (1 Cor 10:13). He gives us milk, not solid food if we are not yet ready for it. (1 Cor. 3:2).

He commands us compassionately "*If it is possible, as much as depends on you, live   peaceably   with all men.*" (Rom. 12:18).

I wish we could learn mercy from the Lord and became merciful.

CHAPTER SIX

"Blessed Are The Pure In Heart For They Shall See God"

A Great Reward:

Purity of heart is certainly valuable, as its reward is very distinguished compared to other rewards and beatitudes.

Concerning other rewards, it is said "For they will be comforted." "For they will inherit the earth" "For they will be filled... For they will be shown mercy."

But in regard to this reward, He says "*For they will see God.*" They will enjoy His companionship. Therfore, the virtue which leads to seeing the Lord must be a great one.

This means that only the pure in heart and the simple can see the Lord, and no one else.

Not Everyone Can See The Lord:

Once saint Serapion converted an adulteress to repentance. He took her away from the place where she used to practise wickedness.

He went to saint Antonios to ask him if God had accepted the woman's repentance. They fasted and prayed for some days to know what God's will for her was. Then it happened that the Lord revealed that matter to saint Paul the Simple, who saw a celebration and many thrones, among which was a great, wonderful empty throne.

There was an angel was charged with presenting saint Paul to those who were present at the celebration. Then, the angel said to Paul, "Who is this empty throne for?" Paul said "It may be for my father Saint Antonios." The angel said "No, it is for the sinful woman who turned from sin through Abba Serapion."

Therefore, we see that God revealed His will to saint Paul because of his simplicity.

We can see through the story of the conversion of Saul of Tarsus that not all people can see the Lord clearly.
Saul saw the Lord Jesus Christ on the way Damascus. But the men who were travelling with him *"hearing the voice but seeing no one."* (Acts 9:7).

Saul heard the voice of the Lord but the Bible says about of travellers who were with him *"My companions saw the light, but they did not hear the voice of Him who spoke to me."* (Acts 22:9).

To see God and hear His voice are spiritual rewards not given to everyone. We see the same case in many parts of the Holy Bible.

God spoke to Samuel the child and did not speak to Eli the priest.

With his pure heart, this child was worthy to have God talk to him and give him a message for Eli (1 Sam 3:1-14). God did not speak directly with Eli because this priest was unworthy as he was under punishment.

Evil people have eyes but they cannot see. They are not worthy of seeing God. This is the greatest punishment for them. They are in the outer darkness (Matt 25:30). Their eyes cannot see the Lord. Their spirits cannot view Him or sense Him.

Concerning our past comments on "seeing God" we mean "Spiritual enjoyment." It has the same meaning when we comment on speaking to God or hearing his voice.

God spoke to the old serpent and punished it. (Genesis 3). He also spoke with devil according to what Job's Book relates. (Job 1,2).

God spoke with Cain and punished him for killing his brother Abel. (Genesis 4).

He also spoke with Satan on the mount of temptation. (Matthew 4).

All that we have mentioned has no connection with spiritual enjoyment because when evildoers meet the Lord, there will be no enjoyment for as the Bible says "*It is a fearful thing to fall into the hands of the living God.*" (Heb 10:31).

It is also said about the second coming: "*Look, He is coming with the clouds and every eye will see Him, even those who pierced Him and all the peoples of the earth will mourn because of Him."* (Rev 1:7).

This means that those who pierced Him will see Him and will mourn because of Him. They will say to the mountains *"Cover us! and to the hills, fall on us* !" (Hos 10:8; Luke 23:30).

The Mind, Simplicity And Tribulations:

The mind that tries to examine everything and to experience all things in the light of its own opinions may be unable to see anything. The opposite of this is the simple person...

You may see God with your spirit more than with your eyes. Your heart, whose vision comes true, may see God. On the contrary, the mind which keeps on examining and wishes to see the Lord according to its own ideas can never see God.

This is why there may be two persons before a spiritual scene, one of them seeing the scenery while the other does not see it.

The simple person, being pure in heart, may probably see, but the closed person in need of God will not.

Seeing God is sometimes connected with pain which purifies the heart.

Because the hearts of the martyrs and confessors were pure and free of temptation and love for the world and were ready to meet the Lord, He would appear to them while they were suffering tortures and horrible pains.

God would appear before the oppressed during their torments and persecution which purified their hearts. This happened to our Father Jacob, the father of fathers, when he escaped from his brother Esau (Gen 28).

During our tribulations we often see the Lord and feel Him work for us, although we do not see Him physically.

David the banished fugitive chants to God and says *"My whole being will exclaim. Who is like You, O' Lord? you rescue the poor from those too strong for them, the poor and the needy from those who rob them."* (Ps 35:10).

He also *says "I foresaw the Lord always before my face. For He is at my right hand, I may not be shaken."* (Acts 2:25). Of course, David did not see the Lord appear before him, but his pure heart felt His presence without seeing according to his own senses. This is why he says ***"Taste and see that the Lord is good"*** (Ps 34:8). Surely, this sight and this taste are beyond the scope of the senses. It is a spiritual enjoyment to see God and enjoy His companionship.

We see Him solving our problems, saving us from our enemies, through every great good and through every blessing. We are at the point of touching God's hand. This is true faith.

Seeing God In Eternity:

The phrase "for they will see God" has another meaning which is: Seeing God in eternity while we are outside the material body. This is what the righteous Job meant when he said "*I know that my Redeemer lives, and He shall stand at last on the earth, and after my skin is destroyed, yet in my own eyes I shall see God*" (Job 19:25-27).

The Holy Bible spoke much of seeing God in eternity. With respect to this subject, Saint Paul the Apostle said: "*For now we see in a mirror dimly, but then face to face.*" (1 Cor 13:12). Then, he continued his words saying "Now, I know in part; then I shall know fully, even as I am fully known."

Here we find the connection between seeing God and knowing Him.

In his second Epistle to the Corinthians, Saint Paul says "*Now the Lord is the Spirit, But we all, with unveiled faces, beholding as in a mirror the glory of the Lord, are being transformed into the same image from glory to glory , just as by the Spirit of the Lord*" (2 Cor 3:17,18).

So we will see God in eternity through spiritual bodies.
When we put off this earthly, corrupt body, and when the perishable wears the imperishable; we are raised in pure spiritual bodies which can see the Lord.

In order to see God, there must be purity of heart. Why is it purity of the heart itself? What will this purity be like? And how can it be attained?

The Purity Of The Heart:

Here, the word "heart" has great importance because the Lord wants your heart itself. He says "*My son, give Me your heart.*" (Ps 23:26). He also, says "*Above all else, guard your heart, for it is the wellspring of life.*" (Ps 4:23).

The Lord Jesus Christ says, "*A good man out of the good treasure of his hear brings forth good, and an evil man out of the evil treasure of his heart brings forth evil.*" (Luke 6:45).

Therefore external purity is not every thing.

Man may keep his senses clean. He commits no sin either through sight or through touching or through hearing and in spite of that, his heart may not be pure.

As Saint Jerome says "There are people who live with celibate bodies but their spirits commit adultery. It means that adultery is in their hearts although their bodies did not commit physical sin.

Also, a person may not make a mistake with his tongue, while his heart is not pure and is filled with anger, hatred, condemnation and revenge. These are exported to his thoughts, which also become polluted.

This is on the negative side, but on the positive side God says "*This people honour Me with their lips but their heart is far from Me.*" (Matt 15:8, Mark 7:6).

God criticised the teachers of the law and Pharisees because *"They prolong their prayers"* (Matt 23:14). In spite of their long prayers, their hearts are far from God.

Of the same quality are the people who abstain from food, subdue themselves and surrender their bodies to flame but have no love in their hearts (1 Cor 13:3). **The pure heart is not only one devoid of sin but one which is filled with God's love.**

All virtues flow from this love, of which God said *"All the law and the prophets hang on it."* (Matt 22:40).

The pure heart begins with the life of repentance.

God says about this purity in the Book of Ezekiel the prophet , *"Cast away from you all the transgression which you have committed, and get yourselves a new heart and a new spirit "* (Eze 18:31). God also says *"I will sprinkle clean water on you, and you shall be clean; I will cleanse you from all your filthiness and from all your idols. I will give you a new heart and put a new spirit within you; I will take the heart of stone out of your flesh and give you a heart of flesh. And I will put My spirit within you and cause you to walk in My statues..."* (Eze 36:25-27).

This is the pure heart which God wants and with which we can see Him. It is the heart which David asked for in his repentance saying, *"Create in me a clean heart, O God, and renew a steadfast spirit within me"* (Ps 51:10).

It is a heart that does not like sin or desire it and does not commit it. So God said, *"My son, give Me your heart"* and immediately after that, *"And let your eyes observe My ways."* (Ps 23:26).

If you give your heart to God, learning the commandments will naturally follow without any exertion, because the pure heart will love virtue and the way to God. It will follow this way with complete satisfaction. A life of righteousness will be its great desire.

The first man was distinguished by purity of heart and simplicity.

Adam and his wife were pure and simple. They were both naked and they felt no shame. (Gen 2:25).

Their hearts were pure and saw no evil in regard to themselves; as the Bible says *"To the pure, all things are pure."* (Tit 1:15).

Consequently, with purity of heart, God wishes us to return to our original state in which He created us, in His likeness and in His image. If we are not able to do that, we at least must come as close to this image as we can.

We shall obtain this purity of heart in eternity. Then we will be like the angels in heaven (Matt 22:30).

With this purity we can see God. Therefore, in our prayers, we say, "O' Lord, if we do not have this purity with which we shall be able to see You, and if we cannot attain such purity, please give it to us as a gift, or give us a taste of this purity and please complete it when we come to Your kingdom in order that we may see You."

The pure heart does not love the world or anything in the world.(1 John 2:15).

Because "*If anyone loves the world, the love of the Father is not in him.*" (1 John 2:15). And "*friendship with the world is enmity towards God.*" (James 4:4).

The person who does not love the world and whose heart has died in regard to friendship with the world, will be filled with God's love only.

There will be no competitor for God in his heart. Like the apostles, he says to the Lord "*We have left everything to follow you*" (Matt 19:27).

The pure hearted man certainly cannot adore two masters. His heart acts for God with equivalent sincerity. If he loves anyone more than Him he will not be worthy of Him (Matt 10:37). So, the heart is purified of any lust and any innocent love becomes enclosed within God's love, not competing with it.

Utterances and words of the pure heart are pure. "*For out of the abundance of the heart, the mouth speaks*" (Luke 6:45). David, the prophet, said "*My heart is stirred by a noble theme.*" (Ps 45:1).

It is not permissible that man becomes very angry and speaks wrongly, then for another to apologise on his behalf, saying, "But his heart is white and clean." The white, clean heart utters clean words and the good man brings good things out of the good stored up in his good heart.

The pure heart is large and can hold everything. It cannot be annoyed by a word or a problem or by any one.

How wonderful the words of St. Paul the Apostle were when he gently blamed the Corinthians and said to them " *O Corinthians! we have spoken openly to you, our heart is wide open. You are not restricted by us, but you are restricted by your own affection .Now in return for the same, I speak as to children. you also be open.*" (2 Cor 6:11-13).

Look at God and see how great His heart is and how it holds everything!

How He causes His sun to rise on the evil and the good. (Matt 5:45). How great His heart is, to let the faithless and idolaters live on earth and to leave the devil without annihilation... !? God's heart is so open to forgiveness that David the prophet says, "*He has not dealt with us according to our sins. Nor punished us according to our iniquities. As far as the east is from the west, so far has He removed our transgressions from us.*" (Ps 103:10,12).

Let us see some examples of pure human beings and how great their hearts are.

The Holy Bible says about Moses the Prophet. *"Now the man Moses was a very humble, more humble than all men who on the face of the earth."* (Num 12:3). And says about Solomon, the Wise *"God gave Solomon wisdom, and exceedingly great understanding, and largeness of heart as like the sand on the seashore."* (1 kin 4:29).

The pure heart undoubtedly has the fruits of the spirit. In regard to this matter, the apostle said *"The fruit of spirit is love, joy, peace, patience, kindness, goodness, faithfulness, gentleness and self-control"* (Gal 5:22,23).

In order that you may see the Lord, you have to acquire all of these qualities.

You may like to read more on the subject of "Purity of heart" in my book "The Life of Repentance and Purity".

If you train your heart to be pure, you will be worthy of the reward "Blessed are the pure in heart, for they will see God."

CHAPTER SEVEN

"Blessed are the peacemakers. For they shall be called sons of God"

The Meaning Of Peacemakers:

Its meaning is threefold: Those who make peace between God and man; those who make peace among people and with God within their own hearts, and those who make peace between the spirit and the body in order that they may not struggle with each other.

1. When peacemakers make peace between God and people, they lead them to faith and repentance and prepare them for the Lord.

About this subject saint Paul the Apostle said *"And he has committed to us the word of reconciliation. Therefore we are ambassadors for Christ, as though God were pleading through us. We implore you on Christ's behalf, be reconciled to God."* (2 Cor 5:18,20).

2. There are two ways to make peace among people. First, we must not cause quarrels among them. If there is any dispute we must not stir it up.

Secondly, we shall play the role of breaking up struggles and bringing love back.

3. As for peace inside ourselves, we must get rid of any internal division or struggle.

Our desires must not contradict our spiritualities; Our thoughts must not be against us. Our hearts must not be in trouble or lost between perplexity and hesitation.

In this chapter, we would like to speak in detail and as much as we can, of the three ways of making peace.

Peace Between God And Man:

Satan is the first creature to raise disputes between God and man.

Through sin and by breaking the commandment, a dispute took place. Hence, the dividing barrier that separated people from the Holy of Holies was created. This is the curtain (Heb 9:3).

It was necessary to pull down this dividing barrier in order to have confidence to enter the Holy of Holies (Heb 10:19).

The burnt offering was made a symbol to satisfy the heart of God, who was angered by our sins. Therefore the whole sacrifice was offered to God alone.

It was forbidden for any one to eat from it. Neither the offerer, nor his friends, nor the priest himself could eat from it;

but the sacrifice had to remain burning on the altar day and night till it was reduced to ashes.

That fire indicated God's justice. But changing the burnt offering to ashes was a symbol of the sacrifice's yielding till the end in order that God's justice might be paid in full (Lev 6:8-13).

Therefore it was said about the burnt offering "*It is a burnt offering, an offering made by fire, an aroma pleasing to the Lord.*" (Lev 1:9,13,17).

There was also the sin offering and the crime offering, which were symbolic of God's justice being paid in full because "*Without the shedding of blood there is no remission.*" (Heb 9:22). Blood was payment in full in return for death as "*The wages of sin is death.*" (Rom 6:23). The blood of animals was a symbol of Christ.

The Lord Jesus Christ performed reconciliation between God and man. This matter was accomplished on the cross through atonement and redemption.

About this subject, the apostle says "*For if when we were enemies, we were reconciled to God through the death of His Son, much more, having been reconciled, we shall be saved through His life!*" (Rom 5:10).

He also said " *Now all things [are] of God, who has reconciled us to Himself through Jesus Christ, ... that is, that God was in Christ reconciling the world to Himself, not imputing their trespasses to them .*" (2 Cor. 5:18,19)}

Saint Paul said "*But now in Christ Jesus you who once were far off have been made near by the blood of Christ. For He Himself is our peace who has made both one and has broken down the middle wall of division between us* " (Eph 2:13-15).

He also said "*making peace through His blood, shed on the cross.*" (Col 1:20).

We thank our Lord Jesus Christ who made peace between God and man, as Son of God, and Son of man.

This is why we call Him the King of Peace and sing to Him saying "O' King of peace, give us Your peace." Isaiah the Prophet says about Him, "*He is the Prince of Peace.*" (Is 9:6).

When the angels announced the good news of His birth, they said "*and on earth peace.*"(Luke 2:14).

Before He made peace, we had been sons of wrath. About this, the apostle says "*You were dead in trespasses and sins ... We were by nature objects of wrath ... He made us alive with Christ even when we were dead in transgression ... And God raised us up together and made us sit together in the heavenly places in Christ Jesus.*" (Eph 2:1-6).

But the Lord Jesus Christ saved us from wrath and reconciled us to God, paying the price on our behalf. So we chant in the Liturgy of St. Gregory saying, "The dividing barrier was destroyed by You and the old hostility done away with. You reconciled the heavenly creation with the earthly, making both one. You perfected the sacrifice through the flesh."

132

The Lord Jesus Christ was the only one to make peace between God and man through atonement and redemption; but we are able to make peace in other ways, such as leading people to the life of faith and repentance.

Jesus said "*I have declared to them Your name, and will declare it. For I have given to them the words which You have given Me.*" (John 17:26,8).

Therefore, we make people know God, love Him, and adhere to His words. We preach to them, perform the ministry of the word of God (Acts 6), the ministry of reconciliation (2 Corinthians 5) and remember the words of the apostle " *He who turns a sinner from the error of his way will save him from death and cover over a multitude of sins* " (James 5:20).

This shows the importance of service, education, looking out for others, private visits, making people love God, religion and the church; as Saint Peter the apostle said, "*for you are receiving the goal, of your faith, the salvation of your souls.*" (1 Peter 1:9).

Jesus Christ is the Son of God. With this authority, He has made peace between God and man. If you behave in the same way, in your own environment, you yourself will be called a "son of God".

If it is so; what can we say about someone who does the opposite? He who causes the others to stumble, and keeps them from the way of the Lord, before whom he will be responsible for their blood.

For example, the one who engenders heresy and heterodoxy; the one who spreads doubt concerning religion, virtue, spirit and immortality ... or the one who leads others to prohibited places, to places of entertainment and emptiness in the name of personal freedom!!

Peace Among People:

The Lord Jesus Christ came and made peace among people. Peace was first made between the Jews and Gentiles, then between Jews and Samaritans.

He came to call the Gentiles to place themselves under God's protection, to do away with the idea of the "chosen people"; to praise both the Gentile centurion and the Canaanite woman, saying that He had not found such great faith even in Israel. (Matt 8:10; Luke 7:9).

He preached in Samaria and said to His disciples *"You shall be witnesses to Me in Jerusalem and in all Judea and Samatia and to the ends of the earth."* (Acts 1:8) *"Go into all the world and preach the gospel to every creation "* (Mark 16:15) *"Go therefore, and make disciples of all nations, baptising them..."* (Matt 28:19).

So we find Paul the Apostle saying to the Gentiles *"Remember that at that time you were without Christ, being aliens from commonwealth of Israel and strangers from the covenants of promise, having no hope. But now you have been by the blood of Christ. Now therefore, you are no longer strangers, but fellow-citizens with saints and members of household of God."* (Eph 2:12-13,19).

He reconciled the Jews with the Samaritans. Concerning this, He taught the parable of the good Samaritan and considered him a true neighbour.

He spoke to the Samaritan woman. He also reconciled those who held fast to religion, while other denominations had despised them such as tax-collectors and sinners.

He taught the parable of the Pharisee and the tax-collector to show them how only the despised tax-collector went home justified before God. (Luke 18:9-14).

He asked us to constantly be in reconciliation with people, even with our enemies and said, *"If anyone wants to sue you and take away your tunic, let him have your cloak also. And whoever compels you to go one mile, go with him two. Love your enemies and pray for those who spitefully use you and persecute you. Do not resist an evil person."* (Matt 5:38-44).

Our teacher Paul the apostle says to us " *Repay no one evil for evil. If it is possible, as much as depends on you, live peaceably with all men. If your enemy hungers, feed him, if he thirsts, give him a drink."* (Rom 12:17-20).

St. Paul himself made peace between Philemon and Onesimus and asked Philemon to deal with him not as a slave, but as a dear brother, saying to him *"If you consider me a partner, welcome him as you would welcome me. If he has done you*

any wrong or owes you. anything, charge it to me. I, Paul, am
writing this with my own hand. I will pay it back." (Phil 16.19).

**Christianity did its best to prevent wars and dissensions.
Saint Paul rebuked the Corinthians when he found there
were discords and disputes among them. (1 Cor 1:10,11).**

Christianity calls us to the life of complete love and to self-
sacrifice. He who hates his brother is considered a killer. It
explains how fleeting the material and worldly matters which
cause disagreement among people are. This is why everyone
must make peace as much as possible.

**Avoiding story telling and bearing criticism from one to
another is one of the most important supports for peace
among people.**

The person who gossips is like a person who sets fire to
people, and plants hatred and malice among them. He certainly
destroys peace. If you have something good to say, say it,
otherwise be quiet. If you hear something bad said by someone
about his brother, be silent as if you have heard nothing.

If you hear of a dispute between two people, try to reconcile
them and bring love back into their hearts. This is why you are
called "son of God".

If the gossiper destroys peace, what can we say about the
person who adds more and more words and agitating
expressions to the original words, or who invents exciting
stories in his own mind to be told to others? Surely, he kindles
fire among them.

136

Such a person cannot be called "son of God". for he is not a peacemaker like Him.

What can we say about the one who reminds another of an old controversy which had been forgotten? Or the one who relates some words said in the past which the other person cannot remember?

But the most amazing thing is that the gossiper thinks that he proves his sincerity while he, in this way, embitters his heart against his brother. He stirs up the water which had been clear and pure.

Don't think that you can acquire other's friendship by attacking his enemies. It is better for you to reconcile two people if you can.

How many disputes have taken place because of this low miserable flattery? ... How many people were forced to take drastic measures against others who had shown no dislike towards them?

The causes of these controversies resemble tribal partisanship. In these disputes, there are no peacemakers at all; consequently, quarrels among the tribes increase.

May all these people remember the words of the Holy Bible "Blessed are the peace-makers for they will be called sons of God."

Internal Peace:

With this peace, you really become a son of God. The bodies of the sons of God are not against their souls but the two live and agree together in God's love. The sons of God are not divided internally. Peace prevails upon their hearts to flow over others.

Of course, the person who lives peacefully with both God and people enjoys internal peace. It is the peace of heart and mind. His conscience is always at ease. His life is full of faith. His heart is calm and secure.

He is neither troubled nor afraid. He suffers no anxiety, Gloominess, perplexity and doubts do not take possession of him.

He leads a peaceful life. He believes that Providence and God's care preserve him. However powerful the evil forces around him are, God is the strongest.

The Lord says "Do not be afraid, for I am with you and no one is going to attack and harm you." (Acts 18:9-10).

If man's faith becomes weak, he will certainly lose his peace and become troubled.

David the prophet kept his internal peace when he was walking through the valley of the shadow of death. (Psalm 23).

The three young men also kept their peace when they were in the fiery furnace.

CHAPTER EIGHT

"Blessed Are Those Who Are Persecuted For Righteousness' Sake"

Our Lord Jesus Christ did not put a paved road carpeted with roses before people, but told them that the road would be hard and the gate would be narrow.

He said to them *"Because the narrow is the gate and difficult is the way which leads to life, and there are few find it"* (Matt 7:14).

He explained to them how they would meet with hardships for the sake of His name and for righteousness' sake.

Then He said to them *"Blessed are those who are persecuted for righteousness' sake , for theirs is the kingdom of heaven." "Blessed are you when they revile persecute you and say all kinds of evil against you falsely for My sake..."* (Matt 5:10-12) See (Luke 6:22,23).

This fact must clear to every Christian. If he behaves righteously, he will suffer.

The Lord Jesus Christ said *"If anyone desires to come after Me, let him deny himself and take up his cross."* (Matt 16: 24).
The Bible also said *"We must through many tribulations enter the kingdom of God."* (Acts 14: 22).

How beautiful the words of Joshua, son of Sirach are. He said to the monk when he ordained him to his office *"My son, if you render yourself to serve God, be ready to face many temptations."*(Sirach 2:1).

He who goes the way of God must be exposed to many hardships in order to know how right his choice of the spiritual way is, and whether he will stand firm in it or not!

There is another cause for these hardships: **devils envy the sons of God for their righteousness, so they trouble them.**

These devils send their attendants to treat them with severity. They place many obstacles before them to force them to turn away from the way of God! They try to make them feel that God's way is too difficult to cross or to remain in.

Devils may send someone to the sons of God to reproach them and ascribe false accusations to them, or send someone who says evil things about them, or someone to insult and persecute them.

The Lord Jesus Christ suffered persecution and dismissal many times.

After Jesus cured the man of Bethesda who had been an invalid for thirty eight years, it was said *"For this reason the Jews persecuted Jesus and sought to kill Him because He had done these things on the Sabbath."* (John 5:16).

141

Once, they refused to welcome Him when He went to a Samaritan village because He was heading for Jerusalem (Luke 9:52,53).

Even in His childhood, when He was in Egypt, they dismissed Him from town to town because the idols fell down before Him in awe" *The idols of Egypt tremble before Him."* (Is 19:1).

Like Jesus Christ, His disciples and many prophets suffered. This is why the Lord Jesus Christ said to His disciples *"But when they persecute you in this city, flee to another."* (Matt 10:23). He also said *"For so , they persecuted the prophets who were before you."* (Matt 5:12).

In the Old Testament, God said of His prophets *"I will send them prophets and apostles, and some of them they will kill persecute."* (Luke 11:49).

He also said *"And some of them you will scourge in your synagogues and persecute from city to city."* (Matt 23:34).

The Lord Jesus Christ told His disciples that they would be persecuted. *"They will lay their hands on you and persecute you. delivering you up to synagogues and prisons and you will be brought before kings and rulers for My name's sake."* (Luke 21:12).

When the man born blind gave good testimony about Christ who had granted him sight, it was said that the Jews insulted Him saying *"You were completely born in sins, and are you teaching us?" "And they cast Him out."* (John 9:30-34).

142

David the righteous prophet was persecuted all his days by king Saul.

It is of great importance for man to be persecuted because of his righteousness and not as the Bible says "*Do not those who plot evil go astray?*" (Ps 14:22).

This is why Saint Peter the Apostle said "*But let none of you suffer as a murderer, thief, an evildoer, or as a busybody in other people's. Yet if any one, suffer as a Christian, let him not be ashamed, but let him glorify God in this matter.*" (1 Peter 4:15,16).

In order to receive this blessing, you must be sure that what happens to you is due to righteousness.

If you are persecuted or insulted or reviled and you deserve what happens to you, owing to your bad behaviour, you will never receive any blessing.

Our teacher, Saint Peter the Apostle explains this saying, "*For this is commendable if because of conscience toward God one endures grief, wrongfully.*" (1 Peter 2:19).

Notice the phrase " *endures grief, wrongfully*", which means that he did nothing worthy of such pains and sorrows.

So the apostle continues his words saying "*For what credit is if when you are beaten for faults, you take it patiently? But when you do good and suffers for it, if you take it patiently, this is commendable before God. For to this you were called, because Christ also suffered for us, leaving us an example, that you should follow in His steps. He committed no sin, and no deceit was found in His mouth."* (1 Peter 2:20-23).

Saint Peter concentrates on these instructions saying ***"But even if you should suffer for righteousness sake , you are blessed... "*** (1 Peter 3:14).

It means that if any harm comes to you for having done good or because of faith, you will be blessed and your reward will be great in heaven...

In this way, prophets were persecuted in the past. Therefore, **you have shared in Christ's pains.**

Because He suffered pains for righteousness and they dismissed Him, reproached Him and said every bad word about Him! The liars !!!! They brought false witnesses against Him and He was numbered with the transgressors (Is 53:120). Then, if you suffer oppression and pain as He did, say with the apostle *"The servant is not like his master"* (Matt 10:24) and *"If they do these things in the tree green wood, what will be done in the dry?"* (Luke 23:31).

Those who persecute you because of your righteousness are undoubtedly compelled by the devil to do so. Therefore, we must not direct our assault toward them, but toward the devil himself.

So, during his struggle against Arius and his followers, Saint Athanasius the Apostolic said "Our first enemy is not Arius but the devil." Through these logical thoughts, we can love our human enemies, as they are not the real enemies.

Our actual enemy is the devil. Human enemies are nothing but victims of the devil who engenders enmity in their hearts. So we have to sympathise with them and pray they are kept safe from him.

This way we understand the meaning of God's commandment which says *"Pray for those who persecute you"* **(Matt 5:44).**

Pray for them in order that the Lord may free them from the devil's domination, save them from their evils and lead them to repentance. Pray for them, because if they get rid of their evils, they will not return to harm you.

And you who are persecuted because of your righteousness, will have your reward in heaven because of your tolerance and your prayers for them. **Even on earth, you will receive help from God.**

After the Jews had persecuted the man born blind and thrown him out of the synagogue, *"Jesus found him"* (John 9:35). God met him because the man needed this meeting. His soul needed someone to support it. So the Lord found him, led him to faith and encouraged him.

Don't think that life with God is mere persecution without sympathy or godly help!!

The spiritual life is not all pains or insults or reproach and persecution, because He says:

"See, I have inscribed you on the palms of My hand." (Is 49:16) *"But the very hairs of your head are all numbered"* (Matt 10:30).

"The sceptre of the wicked will not remain over the land allowed to the righteous, for then the righteous might use their hand to do evil." (Psalm 125). Perhaps it may touch them, but it does not remain over them.

To sum up, we say that the righteous person's life may be: **Pain from people and comfort from God.**

St. Paul the Apostle explains this matter saying *"perplexed, but not in despair, persecuted, but not abandoned, struck down, but not destroyed... Therefore we do not lose heart. Even though our outward man is being renewed day by day."* (2 Cor 4:8,9,16).

Outward persecution is accompanied by inward comfort from God and outward help. This is why, the Lord said *"Blessed are you when people insult you, persecute you and falsely say all kinds of evil against you because of Me."*

The Lord Christ did not only say these words for us , but also followed them Himself. So, the apostle says of Him *"For in that He Himself suffered being tempted, He is able to aid those who are tempted"* (Heb 2:18).

It is also said "*A prophet is not without honour except in his own country.*" (Matt 13:57). They ridiculed Him and with amazement asked "*Where did this Man get these things?*" "*What wisdom is this which is given to Him, that such mighty works are performed by His hands Is this not the carpenter? the Son of Mary. "And they offended at Him."* (Mark 6:2,3) *"When He suffered, , He did not threaten."* (1 Peter 2:23). "*He was oppressed and afflicted, yet He did not open His mouth."* (Is 53:7).

How many insults and criticisms the Lord Jesus Christ endured silently! They said to Him "*Do we not say we rightly that You are a Samaritan and have a demon?*" (John 8:48) and said about Him "*By Beelzebub, the ruler of the demons."* (Luke 11:15) "*Look a gluttonous man and a winebibber, a friend of tax-collectors and sinners*" (Matt 11:19).

They also spoke about Him, saying "*Breaker of the Sabbath. censor of Mosaic law, opponent to Caesar and pervert and misleading."*

During His trial, the high priest said "*He has spoken blasphemy! What further need do we have of witnesses?*" (Matt 26:65).

Also, how easy it is to research the insults and condemnation which the prophets and saints faced!! This subject is so easy that any one of you can investigate it through the Holy Bible or in the Saints' biographies.

147

Perhaps, on this point, our Lord Jesus Christ said *"For in the same way they persecuted the prophets who were before you."* (Matt 5:12).

It was said about Saint Paul, the Apostle, when he stood preaching in Athens *"What is this babbler trying to say?"* (Acts 17:1).

When he spoke about the resurrection they said to him, *"Paul, You are beside yourself!, Much learning is driving you mad!."* (Acts 26:24).

Not all the life of the apostles was glorious, but there was disgrace and contempt in it. So Saint Paul said about both his service and the service of his companions *"By honour and dishonour, by evil report and good report.... As sorrowful, yet always rejoicing."* (2 Cor 6:8,10).

Indeed, it is effective that our fathers the apostles suffered contempt and infamy and were considered deceitful people. They suffered persecution, but were consoled *"Persecuted, but not abandoned."* (2 Cor 4:9). **So, when persecuted, take part in the apostles' pains.** If you do not share in the sanctity which they lived, at least take part in their sufferings.

Saint Peter, the Apostle sympathises with us and says *"Beloved, do not think it strange concerning the { flery} trial which is to try you, as though some strange thing happened to you. But rejoice to extent that you partake of Christ's sufferings that when His glory is revealed."* (1 Peter 4:12,13).

This, then, is participation in the Lord Jesus' sufferings.

About this, Saint Paul said "*I want to know Christ and the power of His resurrection and the fellowship of sharing in His sufferings, becoming like Him in His death.*" (Phil 3:10).

It is partnership in the life of the cross, the cross which we must carry with God or for the sake of God and say with the apostle, "I have been crucified with Christ" (Gal 2:20). But, why that cross? We have to know a true fact: **Evil exists in the world. It works with brutality.**

Weeds still exist among the wheat in the field of God. They will increase and grow until the time of the harvest. (Matt 13:30).

Light as well as darkness exists in the world. When God created light, He did not say "*Let there be no darkness*" but said "*Let there be light.*" Darkness remained and reigned. So, Jesus Christ said to the Jews "*But this is your hour. when darkness reigns.*" (Luke 22:53).

So, evil powers exist and fight against the good and against righteousness. Sometimes they are more powerful because their means are limitless.

The righteous person is bound with restrictions such as truthfulness and good, but the evil one can tell lies, deceive, delude, intrigue, and weave plots and conspiracies. He can do harm, take revenge, threaten and reveal secrets ...

The righteous one cannot commit any of these vices. The two scales therefore seem imbalanced.

Evil may triumph at first but the righteous person will endure many deceptive things because of his righteousness, and remain in his sufferings till Providence saves him.

Examples Of Righteous People :

There was of a physician who worked in a public hospital. He was righteous and did not want to use his position to gain illegal advantage.

This physician had replaced someone accustomed to referring patients to his own clinic, especially those patients in need of surgery, and would sell them drugs and medicines which were given free of charge at the hospital. As would be expected, the righteous physician refused to follow the evil way.

A peasant came to the upright physician and asked him to perform an operation on him and presented a sum of money, but the surgeon refused to take the money. The farmer thought that the man found the sum too small, so he presented more and more money, but the surgeon would not take any money from the farmer and convinced him that the hospital treats people free of charge, and the man went on his own way.

Meanwhile, a male nurse became angry because of the doctor's behaviour and said to him: "Why did you tell the peasant that hospital treatment is free of charge?" "Why do you want to reduce our income?" "Don't you know that any peasant you perform an operation on is accustomed to give us a sum of money?" "In this way we shall receive no income at all!"

Complaints against the physician followed one after the other. They accused him of being a Communist and of working against the government. He paid the price for his honesty and righteousness. They also tried to transfer him to another hospital far away. This person is counted among "Those persecuted for their righteousness."

The Example Of Joseph The Righteous   He refused to commit adultery with his master's wife. She falsely accused him of trying to seduce her.   She succeeded in damaging his reputation. Consequently he was dismissed from the house and from his post.   Then he was put in prison. (Genesis 39). Therefore, he received this beatitude *"Blessed are those who are persecuted because of righteousness"*.

He certainly suffered persecution because of his righteousness. Evil succeeded at the beginning of the battle, but God did not leave him.   In the end he was appointed Prime Minister of the kingdom.   He also became father to a Pharaoh, lord of his entire household and ruler of Egypt. (Gen 45:8).

It was as if an angel whispered the words of the Lord in Joseph's ear *"Blessed are you when they revile and, persecute you and say all kinds of evil against you falsely for My sake. Rejoice and be exceedingly glad, for great is your reward in heaven."* (Matt 5:11,12).

Not only did Joseph obtain his reward in heaven but he also received it on earth. He is counted among the saints within the history of salvation.

There is example of an accountant, who refused to falsify accounts. If he refused to do this, the owner of the company would dismiss him. Then, he would be persecuted for his righteousness. But as Malachi, the Prophet says: "*And the Lord listened and heard them. So a book of remembrance was written before Him.*" (Mal 3:16). God does not forget the righteousness of those who are godly.

The Lord sees their deeds and rewards each one according to what he does. God, whose name is blessed, knows the price paid by the pious one to hold on to their righteousness... **Thus, the righteous person is exposed to great suffering by evildoers.**

Here is the singer chanting in his Psalm "*They have greatly oppressed me from my youth; they have greatly oppressed me from my youth. Ploughmen have ploughed my back and made my furrows long.*" (Psalm 128).

Here we notice that they did not just plough his back, but also continued to lash him for a long time. But the Lord saved him at last as he says "*The Lord is righteous; He has cut me free from the cords of the wicked.*", yet the wicked continue to do harm to the righteous.

The righteous cannot reply to the wicked with the same insults. They cannot exchange outrage with them, or deceit or fights because their consciences cannot allow them to do so.

They cannot take revenge for themselves according to God's will, (Rom 12:19) but turn the other cheek, go the second mile and leave the cloak to the one who wants to take the tunic (Matt 5:39-41).

They silently bear all this wickedness until the Lord interferes and treats them with justice. *"Who executes justice for the oppressed."* (Ps 146:7).

Moses said about the Lord *"The Lord will fight for you; you shall hold your peace."* (Ex 14:14).

In spite of all these sufferings, the righteous are doubtless far better than their persecutors.

Those who persecute others are poor because they really persecute themselves. They lose their purity of heart as well as their eternity. They lose God himself, as He opposes their oppression. They lose their reputation. Because of their evil deeds people get a bad idea about them. They may fall because of their evils, even after a time.

History tells us strange stories about how the lives of those persecutors ended. **God supports both the oppressed and the persecuted on earth and in heaven.**

Throughout his life, he enjoys purity of heart. His conscience does not rebuke him for anything. Oppression itself strengthens the relationship with God and deepens his prayers and his fasting and covers him with spirituality. He experiences the life of faith and how the Lord stretches His hand into his life and saves him. He will receive a great reward in heaven for what he endures on earth.

Keeping his inner peace is very important to him and he chants with the singer "*Though an army encamp against me, my heart shall not fear.*" (Ps 27:3).

A person's attachment to heaven makes him endure suffering with self-satisfaction.

How gentle the words of Saint Paul the apostle, are: "*If in this life only we have hope in Christ, we are of all men the most pitiable.*" (1 Cor 15:19).

We suffer on earth while the sinners enjoy its pleasures. But we are unhappy on earth because we look forward to the enjoyment of heaven, and know well the words our father Abraham said to the rich man and Lazarus "*Son, remember that in your lifetime you received your good things, and likewise Lazarus evil things, but now he is comforted and you are tormented*" (Luke 16:25).

Thus, we must pay attention to the heavenly reward because it is more important, more continuous and is everlasting.

The first man banished because of sin was our father Adam and with him was our mother Eve. God banished them from the

Garden of Eden and prevented them from approaching the tree of life   (Gen 3:23,24).

The first man banished for his righteousness was the righteous Abel.

Cain banished him from the earth. He attacked Abel and killed him because Abel was righteous. *"By faith Able offered to God a more excellent sacrifice than Cain. Through which he obtained witness that he was righteous, when God testifying of his gift"* (Heb 11:4).

The number of saints persecuted for their righteousness increased. Their biographies are mentioned in the Holy Bible and the "Fathers' Biography".

We are going to mention some of them in order that we may receive consolation when we meet with some of their sufferings.

Models Of Saints Banished And Persecuted:

• **David the Prophet:**

Before God and people, David was a righteous man. The Lord chose him from amongst his seven brothers who were older than him. So Samuel took the horn of oil and anointed him in the presence of his brothers (1 Sam 16:13). **David became anointed for God and the Spirit of the Lord came upon him.**

At the same time the Spirit of the Lord had departed from Saul, and an evil spirit from the Lord tormented him (1 Sam 16:14). He needed David to dismiss the evil spirit from him; this is the report given to Saul about David: "*He is skilful in playing the harp. A mighty man of valour, a man of war, prudent in speech and a handsome person. And the Lord is with him*" (1 Sam 16:18). **David succeeded in forcing the evil spirit to leave Saul. (1 Sam 16:23).**

This was proof that David was a righteous man, and that the Lord was with him. Also, the great ability of David to kill the champion Goliath proved his faith and his righteousness and that God was with him. Moreover, killing the lion and the bear (1 Sam 17:27) proved that the Lord was with him as the Lord saved David from them. In spite of all this, David suffered bitter persecution from Saul because the Lord supported him!

The Bible says "*Thus Saul saw and knew that the Lord was with David... Saul was still more afraid of David, So Saul became David's enemy continually*" (1 Sam 18:28,29).

Many times Saul tried to kill David "*Saul spoke to Jonathan his son and to all his servants that they should kill David*" (1 Sam 19:1) "*Saul sought to pin David to the wall with the spear but he slipped away from Saul's presence.*" (1 Sam 19.10).

David remained fugitive and escaped from Saul from desert to desert. He went to Samuel at Ramah, then he and Samuel went to Naioth. Saul sent men to capture David (1 Sam 19:18).

Then, David fled from Naioth and went to his friend Jonathan, the son of Saul, and said to him *"What have I done? What is my iniquity? and what is my sin before your father, that he seeks my life!?"* (1 Sam 20:1).

David went to Nob, to Aheimelech the priest (1 Sam 21:1) Saul continued to persecute him and he went to Achish king of Gath (1 Sam 21:10).

David left Gath and escaped to the cave of Adullam. (1 Sam 22:1). Then he went to Mizpah in Moab; then to the forest of Hereth (1 Sam 22:3,5); then to Keilah. (1 Sam. 23:1).

In all these persecutions we read a comforting phrase: about David: "Banished because of his righteousness.": " *Saul sought him every day , but God did not deliver him into his hands."* (1 Sam 23:14).

David escaped to the Desert of Ziph ... then to En-Gedi (1 Sam 23:15,29). Saul pursued him, but David escaped to the Desert of Moan. (1 Sam 25:1).

After a series of persecutions, David was saved and Saul died, but not at David's hand.

David the righteous suffered many rejections from people other than King Saul. His banishment was a blessing to him and to us.

This banishment helped David to practise the life of modesty and repentance.

If not for him, some of his sweet and comforting psalms, named by some people as "Songs of the banished one" would not have been sung.

If it were not for his banishment, he would not have lived in the deep faith through which he felt the hand of the Lord stretched to save him and help him.

He said with all his heart *"We have escaped like a bird out of the fowler's snare; the snare has been broken, and we have escaped. Praise be to the Lord, who has not let us be torn by their teeth."*(Psalm 124).

• **Paul the Apostle**

Saint Paul, the Apostle, the great righteous man, who worked harder than all of the saints in preaching the Gospel and in teaching, (1 Cor 1 5:10) was banished for his righteousness.

He suffered bitterly when he was in Philippi because of a miracle done by the Lord through him ... !

There was a slave girl who had a spirit through which she predicted the future. Her masters made much money through her predictions. In the name of Jesus Christ, Paul the Apostle drove that evil spirit out of the slave girl. When her owners realised that their hope of making money was gone, they seized Paul and his companion Silas and dragged them into the market-place to face the authorities.

They were thrown into prison till the magistrates came to appease them and escorted them from prison, requesting them to leave the city. Thus, the Lord saved them,(Acts 16:16-39).

At Ephesus, Paul suffered the same persecution because of his righteousness. His preaching the Gospel was a great disaster to the craftsmen who made idols. At Ephesus, there was the temple of the goddess Artemis whose statue was believed to have descended from Zephes (heaven).

Saint Paul could attract many people to faith. He told them that man-made gods were no gods at all. The assembly was in confusion. There was a great demonstration. All the people said "Great is Artemis of the Ephesians! " *Then Paul left Ephesus for Macedonia* "(Acts 19:23-20:1).

Not only was Paul rejected, but all the Christians also: Even before saint Paul's preaching we hear of the first church that, "*A great persecution arose against the church which was at Jerusalem and they were all scattered throughout the regions of Judea and Samaria*". (Acts 8:1).

The Lord employed this scattering for the benefit of Christianity. Here we read that everlasting phrase in which divine inspiration says *"Those who were scattered went everywhere preached the word."* (Acts 8:4).

Thus, the Lord changed evil into good ... Blessed are those who were persecuted because of righteousness.

- **Jeremiah, the prophet.**

Jeremiah, the great one to whom the Lord said *"Before I formed you in the womb I knew you, before you were born I set you apart. I appointed you as a prophet to the nations."* **(Jer 1:5) was banished because of righteousness. The people of his time were so depraved that they did not accept his mission. Thus, he was persecuted bitterly.**

He said to God pleadingly " *Righteous are You , O' Lord, when I plead with You. Yet lat me talk with You about Your judgements. Why does the way of the wicked prosper!? Why are those happy who deal so treacherously?"* (Jer 12: 1).

Jeremiah faced the contention of people because of his prophecies. They cursed him and attacked his prophetic deeds so severely that he said *"Woe is me my mother, that you have borne me , a man of strife and a man of contention to the whole earth. Everyone curses me"* (Jer 15:10).

Jeremiah complained to the Lord of the injustice occurring to him.

He said *"for they have dug a pit to capture me and have hidden snares for my feet. But You know, O' Lord, all their plots to kill me."* (Jer 18:22,23). He also said *"I am in derision daily; everyone mocks me.. So the word of the Lord was made to me a reproach and a derision daily."* (Jer 20:7,8).

In the end Jeremiah was thrown into the dungeon and he sank down into the mud.

They had him beaten and imprisoned him (Jer 37:15,21). This happened according to the orders of king Zedekiah. Because Jeremiah was honest in regard to his prophecy, and did not flatter the king or the chiefs or the people; they took him and put him into the cistern of the king's son which was in the court-yard of the guard "*They lowered Jeremiah by ropes into the cistern.*"

It had no water in it, only mud, and Jeremiah sank down into the mud. (Jer 38:6).

He stayed there until they lifted him out of the cistern. And Jeremiah remained in the courtyard of the guard.

• **Micah the prophet:**

Micah the prophet faced the same problem for the same reason as Jeremiah the prophet did, because he refused to flatter the king of Israel saying "*As surely as the Lord lives, I can tell him only what the Lord tells me*"(1 Kin 22:14). Then he said his prophecy, but the king was not satisfied with what he had heard and said "*Put the fellow in prison and give him nothing but bread and water*" (1 Kin 22:27).

• **Saint Athanasius the Apostolic:**

Many times, Saint Athanasius suffered banishment, persecution and being made an outcast because of his righteousness and defense of the faith.

He was banished from his episcopal seat four times. He lived many years driven away; roaming from one country to another, between east and west.

The Arians revolted against him, held meetings against him, accused him falsely, stirred up the authorities against him. This well known phrase was said to him "Athanasius, the whole world is against you."

The same words can be said about many patriarchs.

Saint Dioscorus, for example, was banished from his episcopal seat for defending the faith. There were also those who followed that saint for a period of 190 years from the Chalcedon Period till the Arabs came to Egypt (641-644 AD). When Amr-ibn-el As came to Egypt, Pope Benjamin was banished from his episcopal seat for more than thirteen years, roaming from town to town and from one village to another, confirming people in faith.

In the days of Gostinian, at the beginning of the sixth century, Saint Severus the patriarch of Antioch was exiled because of his righteousness. He was banished from his episcopal seat for nearly 28 years which he spent in Egypt.

Rejoice And Be Glad:

The Lord concluded the beatitude "Blessed are those who are persecuted because of righteousness" saying, "*Rejoice and be exceedingly glad, for great is your reward in heaven, for so they persecuted the prophets who were before you."* (Matt 5:12).

We have given examples of "Prophets' persecution and banishment."

The Lord did not only say "Endure" about persecution, but he also said "Rejoice and be glad."

Rejoice for the crowns prepared for you; for the paradise waiting for you in eternity. Rejoice because you have chosen the right way; the narrow road that leads to life (Matt 7:14).

You have carried the cross as your master did. Yes, rejoice for the fathers, the prophets did the same when they flogged them, then released them.

The Bible says *" So they departed from the presence of the council, rejoicing that they were counted worthy to suffer shame for His name. "* (Acts 5:41).

CHAPTER NINE

"You Are The Salt Of The Earth, You Are The Light Of The World"

A Wonderful Order:

In fact, the beatitudes seem to be given by God to us in a wonderful order. The first thing that attracts our attention is that the Lord has made meekness and modesty a basis for the whole spiritual life. He said "*Blessed are the poor in spirit, blessed are the meek.*"

For the person who does not build his life on modesty, all virtues will be food for worthless glory and pride.

But whatever height the person who is poor in spirit may reach in spiritual improvement, his heart does not feel haughty because it is inwardly crushed.

Thus, his humility will form a strong fence around his virtues. So he keeps them in safety.

If a person keeps his virtues and attains purity of heart and peace between himself and the Lord, devils will envy him and stir persecution up against him because of his righteousness.

Thus, after the Lord had said "Blessed are the pure in heart" "Blessed are the peace-makers", He said *"Blessed are those who are persecuted because of righteousness."*

If a spiritual man endures any persecution, he will rejoice because he carries the cross of Christ and will receive a great reward in heaven.

Not only is the spiritual life a religious war for keeping the heart pure, but it also has another function for the sake of others.

Thus, after the Lord had explained all the beatitudes, He said "You are the salt of the earth; you are the light of the world." *"Let your light so shine before men, that they may see you good works and glorify your Father in heaven."* (Matt 5:13-16).. **Here, the Lord shows us that we must not be satisfied with personal virtues, but have a mission towards others.**

The phrases "poverty in spirit, meekness, purity of heart" express personal virtues. Then, our mission is:

"You Are The Salt Of The Earth."

Food cannot taste good without salt. Salt gives it good flavour. The Lord even says of offerings in Leviticus: *"And every offering of your grain offering you shall season with salt. You shall not allow the salt of covenant of your God to be lacking from your grain offerings, With all your offerings you shall offer salt"* (Lev 2:13).

Here the Lord says "*You are the salt of the earth*;" I have put you on the whole earth in order that you may repair and mend it to give it a good taste.

No one can relinquish his responsibility towards others and say the words of Cain "*Am I my brother's keeper?*" (Gen 4:9).

Certainly, you are your brother's keeper. If you truly love him, your love will force you to keep him from both material dangers and spiritual errors through your meek and spiritual way.

Thus, the apostle said "*Brethren, if a man is overtaken in any trespass, you who are spiritual restore such a one in a spirit of gentleness...Bear one another's burdens, and so fulfil the law of Christ.*" (Gal 6:1,2). **So, as far as you can, you are responsible for others**.

You are responsible for doing something good for people in the environment you live in.

If you have lived with Christ and tasted His sweetness, you are supposed to say the words of David the Prophet to people, "*Taste and see that the Lord is good.*" (Ps 34:8).

Say this phrase to those who listen to you or taste its flavour through your life. And as you have reached God, let others go with you in order that they may taste His sweetness.

166

Although the Samaritan woman had recently turned away from sin yet, no sooner had she known Christ than she went and announced the good news to the people. *"Many of the Samaritans of that city believed in Him because of the word of the woman who testified."* (John 4:39). If she had kept silent no one would have blamed her, but she could not be silent.

Anyone who knows the Lord cannot remain silent. The high priests and the elders tried all means to silence the disciples but they could not. These holy men answered them saying, *"For we cannot but speak the things which we have seen and heard."* (Acts 4: 20).

Ask yourself then, "Are you the salt of the earth and the light of the world?" "What have you done for others?"

The church, as a group of saints who behave according to the eminent principles of Christ, must perform a mission to the world. These principles reach and spread all over the world through those saints. How can this be accomplished in respect to the church as a whole and to you as an individual?

The Mission Of Being A Model:

It is supposed that our living among people can be a model to them; an example set before them, in which they find the practical way to the life of faith and purity. Yes, it is our duty to present the image of God to people as Christ presented it to us.

Redemption was the main cause of Christ's incarnation; but one of the other causes was that humanity lost the divine image. So the Lord Christ came to reveal God's image to humanity so that they could live according to it.

Look at the Jesus Christ, when He washed the feet of His disciples and said to them "*If I then , your Lord and Teacher, have washed your feet, you also ought to wash one another's feet. I have given to you an example that you should do as I have done to you.*" (John 13:14,15).

Thus Saint Peter said to us about Jesus Christ " *leaving us an example, that you should follow His steps.* " (1 Pet 2:21).

In the same way, Saint Paul, the Apostle said "*Follow my example, as I follow the example of Christ.*" (1 Cor 11:1).

In this way, our fathers the apostles were the light of the world. They were examples to others.

Thus, in more than one place, the apostle urges his sons to imitate him (1 Cor 4:16); (2 Thess 3:9) "*and note those who so walk, as you have us for a patterns.*" (Phil 3:17).

No one can find his way in darkness, but in light, he can see it. Thus, the mission of saints, who are the light of the world, is to show people the way to God, and to be their examples in following that way, till they reach *"that they may see your good works and glorify your Father in heaven."* (Matt 5:16).

Life, as an example, is a biblical commandment. Saint Paul, the Apostle, says to his disciple Timothy " *Let noone* *despise your youth, but be an example to the believers in word, in conduct, in love, in spirit, in faith and in purity.*"(1 Tim 4:12).

He says to his disciple Titus "*In everything set them an example by doing what is good.*" (Titus 2:7).

Perhaps not everyone has the ability and the capacity to teach; for teaching is entrusted to those who are effective and good.

But they can be an example for all people. Anyone can follow them. He who is unable to preach can be an example to others through his behaviour.

A sermon teaches theoretically, while the example presents practical lessons.

About this, the apostle says "*You are our epistle... known and read by all men. You are manifestly an epistle of Christ, ministered by us*" (2 Cor 3:2,3).

He also says that the Lord Jesus Christ "*through us diffuses the fragrance of His knowledge. For we are to God the fragrance of Christ.*" (2 Cor 2:14,15).

It is expected that anyone who sees us benefits from our manner even without conversing with us, and benefits from our style of speech and in our behaviour without need for preaching.

On one hand, it is well known that people benefit by others' lives more than profiting by their words. On the other hand, if the preacher's behaviour is not spiritual his sermons will not be fruitful or useful to people. **The example is also useful in regard to those to whom you cannot preach.**

You may advise, preach to or teach those who are younger than you, or those who are less intellectual or in less standing than you; but you may be embarrassed to advise or preach to those who are superior to you. Such people can make use of the following examples.

There are people who do not tolerate or accept preaching. Their pride and their self-assertion prevent them from the acceptance of advice or a word which draws their attention to the right way, or a word to teach or preach to them. Nor can they endure a word of criticism.

If you speak a word of benefit, he may look at you, show his resentment and say to you "Are you going to preach to me?" Such persons may benefit more from your good example, which will speak to them in silence.

Regarding the necessity of examples, the Apostle says "*Be careful to do what is right in the eyes of everybody.*" (Rom 12:17). He gives more explanation and says "*Providing honourable things not only in the sight of the Lord but also in the sight of men.*" (2 Cor 8:21).

In this way, the believer's life becomes a light to others. **To become a light has three advantages:**

1. A person becomes of great use to others because he presents a practical and spiritual example to them.

2. On the other hand, he will not be a stumbling-block to anyone.

3. This good behaviour will lead people to glorify our Heavenly Father, according to the Lord's words.

Therefore, "If you behave well, you will make people love their religion." If you behave badly, people will blaspheme God because of you.

Moreover, James, the Apostle says "*Do they not blaspheme that noble name by which you are called?*" (James 2:7).

The following is an important note which we add with respect to those who are salt and light of the world.

An Example Even After Death:

The pious person is the salt of the earth during his life as well as after his death, because people will follow his steps afterwards. He will remain an example for future generations.

Saint James, the Apostle, says "*Brethren, take the prophets, who spoke in the name of the Lord, as an example of suffering and patience. You have heard of Job's perseverance and seen the end intended by the Lord.*" (James 5:10,11). When our teacher St. James used this example, Job the righteous had passed away thousands of years before. In spite of the passage of time, he remains a good example in the present as the salt of the earth and light of the world.

The spiritual person shines like a light. His life extends through future generations. After his death, his biography remains shining before people.

Look how our fathers the monks were the salt of the earth and the light of the world!! People came from the most distant countries to hear a word of benefit from their mouths.

After their death, their sanctified biographies have shone all over the world giving people wisdom, and spiritual understanding, even in the present.

I wonder if Saint Antonios' life has come to an end? Surely not. He is still alive. He preaches, speaks and clarifies the way through his biography, as it was said about Abel the righteous " ... *and by faith he still speaks, even though he is dead.*" (Heb 11:4).

The same words can be said about St. Augustine. In his contemplations, he was a light and in present times he still shines.

Through his sermons, St. John Chrysostom was a light and still shines. Also, the other saints shine through their teachings and biographies. Thus, the apostle says: "*Remember those who rule you, who spoke the word of God to you. Considering the outcome of their conduct imitate*" (Heb 13:7).

As to whether examples can have a negative or positive effect, we refer to the story of Ghandi.

This great Indian leader was greatly touched by Christian doctrine. It is said that when he visited France, he stood before the icon of the crucified Lord and wept. He used to say his famous words "I love Christianity but ... "

Some Christians at that time had behaved unpleasantly and had an unsightly manner, Christian rulers in South Africa who severely persecuted coloured people, and other Christian rulers who settled in Indian colonies and ruled there with unsurpassed cruelty. Thus, they gave the worst possible image of Christian rule.

If , at that time, the Christian rulers, both in India and South Africa had had a spiritual standard, Ghandi would have been touched by Christianity and the 400 million Indians would have followed him as well.

On the contrary, Ghandi, the Brahman, was a living and spiritual ideal in his days. He was above all Christians; if he abstained from food he could shake the English Parliament. Because of his endurance and willingness to bear pain, he won the admiration of the people especially in the Christian world.

He faced persecution without any struggle or revenge.

He pronounced curses on the cruel and oppressive rulers who were Christian by name yet a terrible picture of Christianity in reality.

One good example is Abba Antonius.

Saint Athanasius, the Apostolic, said about him: "As soon as the troubled, the perplexed and the bitter in spirit saw Abba Antonius' face, their hearts were filled with peace."

Such was the extent of the impression of those saints about whom the Holy Bible said "You are the light of the world; you are the salt of the earth."

One of the examples who had an impression on me was Archdeacon Habib Girgis. Our teacher the archdeacon Habib Girgis was not only the teacher of his generation, but was also an ideal person.

Every time I visited him, I used to hear a word of benefit from his mouth and would write it in my note-book. When I saw his meekness and his good heart I used to say to myself "If one human being has such humility, how much more lamb-like would our Lord be!!

In this way, I left glorifying God through the personality of that man.

Thus, if any spiritual meaning seems difficult to understand it can be seen practically in man.

For example, if we do not understand the meaning of the word "meekness", we can see it, in detail, in the meek. Thus, the spiritual sons of God become the means of explanation of all virtues which people can learn through their countenance even if they do not speak or preach.

Why Salt And Light In Particular?

You are the salt with which the world is mended. The salt seasons the world and makes it pleasant and agreeable. You are the light which illuminates the way to God. Here, the Lord raises the morale of His audience, saying that they are blessings and menders of the world. And furthermore that they are a town on a hill; a lamp on its stand which gives light to all people.

The sermon on the mount begins with beatitudes. Then with words of praise and encouragement with which He strengthens their feeble arms and weak knees. (Heb 12:12) as if He were to say to them, "**You are not unknown. The whole world acknowledges and feels your existence.**"

If a man tastes some food he can taste and know the quantity of salt in it, whether it is small or large or of moderate quantity.

The same case is applied to the true Christian. If he is found in any society or gathering, those around him will feel his presence and his impact and as some think that the pure hearted Christian has to live in society unremembered, unknown and perceived by none.

Self-denial in a life of modesty differs from one's impression on others.

Saint Paul the Apostle was loved by many people. Some became his disciples but others wished to kill him. He made his presence felt and all acknowledged him.

When John the Baptist came out of the wilderness and appeared before people, he made his presence felt among them. He had a great impression on them in spite of his self denial.

It is possible that man can deny himself, yet at the same time, no one can deny his spiritual effect on the society in which he lives.

Words Of Praise:

How wonderful is Christ's love which makes Him praise dust and ashes

Although He knows the weakness of humanity He encourages the timid (1 Thess 5:14). He praises human beings although their conduct is like a woman's monthly uncleanness in His sight. (Ezek 36:17). God said to us "*So likewise you, when you have done all those things which you are commanded, say, "We are unprofitable servants, we have only what was our duty to do*" (Luke 17:10). Despite this, He says to us "You are the salt of the earth. You are the light of the world".

Even though He said this about His disciples, He knew their weaknesses and that they would escape and leave Him alone at the time of His crucifixion. He knew who would deny Him, who would be afraid, who would believe Him to be a ghost on the day of Resurrection, and who would be filled with doubt. In spite of all that He says "You are the salt of the earth. You are the light of the world."

He said this about the ignorant of the world whom He would use to shame the wise. He said this about the weak whom he would use to shame the strong.

He also said this about those whom He described as "*The weak things of this world, to put to shame the things which are mighty* " (1 Cor 1:27,28).

God is amazing in regard to His love, His encouragement and to His praising human beings, His sons.

God was proud of His servant Job. He said to Satan, "*Have you considered My servant Job, that there is none like him on the earth; a blameless and upright man who fears God and shuns evil?*" (Job 1:8). He repeated this praise once more and added that Job "*still he holds fast to his integrity.*" (Job 2:3). even though the Lord knew Job's weaknesses (Job 40:8).

The Lord raises morals but the human beings do not do so!

God, who is perfect in everything and unlimited in His perfection, endures the weaknesses of people. *"A bruised reed He will not break, and smoking flax He will not quench."* (Is 42:3).

But people cannot bear each other's weaknesses, even though they are susceptible to slipping and failing.

The Importance Of Salt:

Salt is a very necessary thing. We cannot dispense with it. In fact, salt is more important and more useful than sugar. You cannot dispense with salt, but sometimes you can dispense with sugar. It is well known that starchy substances are converted to sugar in the body.

Sometimes you can dispense with some starchy substances as well. But salt is a fundamental and indispensable substance. For example, in your house, you can dispense with some furniture, portraits and pieces, but you cannot dispense with water. It is something as fundamental as salt.

Man can dispense with eating meat and costly fruit, but he cannot dispense with salt.

Sometimes, when anyone wishes to describe his harmony and his true attachment to others he says "We have eaten bread and salt together."

It was even necessary to season the offerings with salt. (Lev 2:13).

Although salt is very necessary, it is also very cheap. Anyone can get it because it is cheap and available. Its importance is not due to its value but to its necessity. This can be said about the sons of God who are in the world. Some of them may be fishermen or tent-makers, or shepherds and at the same time they are of great importance to the world. The gospel should reach them. **Thus the sons of God are necessary and available**.

178

They are the salt whom the world cannot dispense with. The world has no taste and is useless without them. The world can not only be mended by priests, men of religion and preachers, but also with all believers. The Lord said these words to all people when He gave His sermon on the mount.

The important thing is not our post or our position, but our effectiveness and fruitfulness.

The sight of Saint Elisha the Prophet was so disturbing that some youths came out of the town and jeered at him saying, "*You, baldhead, you, baldhead*" (2 Kin 2:23). In spite of that, he performed miracles and raised the dead. He was light and salt to his generation. The kings considered him a father and guide. (2 Kin 13:14).

The manner of Saint Roweis caused people to scoff at him. Some thought him insane, but he was a blessing to his generation. He performed many miracles. His light still shines in present times.

We may ask, 'To whom did the Lord say "You are the salt of the earth." '

Of course, He meant those whom He praised in His sermon on the mount: the poor in spirit, the meek, the merciful, the pure in heart and the peace-makers ... and not only the preachers and the teachers ... because religion is not mere words but it is spirit and it is life (John 6:63).

With such the world is mended. If preachers wish to be the salt of the earth, let them be adorned with the Beatitudes.

Priests and preachers are numerous, but their impression does not compare with one like Paul, the Apostle, because God does not preach through them as He did through Paul or perhaps they are mere preachers and not a light.

We must not blame the church or its servants, because every one of you is responsible for it and ought to say with Joshua the Prophet, *"But as for me and my house, we will serve the Lord."* (Josh 24 :15).

If each family takes a spiritual interest in regard to its children, we shall not need preachers or instructors or teachers to teach religion.

If parents become a light to their sons and daughters and behave according to the instructions of the Lord Jesus Christ, the church will be filled with saints.

I say these words to those who bring their sons to the church to be baptised.

We give as an example: Moses' mother and her influence on him.

Saint Jochebed, Moses' mother (Ex 6:20), took him from Pharaoh's daughter when he was three months old. She suckled him not only milk from her breast but also faith and the true creed. When he grew, she took him to Pharaoh's daughter and he became her son. (Ex 2:10).

How many years did Moses spend with his mother? Three, four, five years!! However short the period, he received faith which remained with him all his life when he was in the princess' palace surrounded by the Pharaonic worship of idols - the gods of ancient Egyptians. Moses did not only remain faithful but became the pioneer of faith in his age, and the presenter of it to all future generations.

Blessed is Saint Jochebed because she was light and salt.

On this subject, I remember that I once I saw a duck which had incubated its eggs until they hatched. Then it began to walk surrounded by twenty ducklings, very pleased with them. The scene was delightful. It seemed as if it were singing with the prophet, *"Here am I, and the children whom the Lord has given me."* (Is 8:18).

We ask you, "Who are the children you will present to God when you stand before Him on the dreadful judgement day in order that you may enter into partnership with the Lord Jesus Christ? *"In bringing many sons to glory?"* (Heb 2:10,13).

Will you stand alone, on that day, as a branch without fruit?

Recall to mind the Parable of the Talents, when the man who had received five talents came to the Lord and said *"Master, you delivered to me five talents. Look, I have gained five more talents beside them."* Then he was worthy of hearing the phrase *"Well done, good and faithful servant! You were faithful over a few things, I will make you ruler of many things. Enter into the joy of your lord."*

The man with the two talents did the same thing. (Matt 25:20-23).

I marvel at these few persons who can change the occurrences of the world spiritually.

I have a high opinion of the twelve apostles and St. Paul whose voices went out over all the earth. (Ps 19:4).

I am astonished that such a few Old Testament prophets spread faith through those generations.

They were so few in number, but they were the light of the world and the salt of the earth.

Through them, generations became distinguished from others.

Thus we say : This is the generation of Elijah and that is the generation of Elisha.

So each generation had its light, to whom the Lord had entrusted its guidance.

In this way we say "This is the age of Jeremiah and those were the days of Samuel and David ..."

What we say about the ages of prophets and apostles, we say about history also.

This also happened in the days of Saint Athanasius, or the days of Saint Kyrollos (Cyril), or the age of Saint Antonius, the Great, or in the days of Abba Abram, the Bishop of Fayoum.

All of them were a light to their generations and to future generations. Indeed they were fruitful.

Believe me, we learn a good lesson from the wheat seed.

We plant it in the ground; then it sprouts and gives us plenty of corn *"first the blade, then the head, after that the full grain in the head"* (Mark 4:28).

All these grains come from one seed. The same case corresponds with the palm-tree which continually gives us dates.

How much doesa fruitful tree yield every season?

And you! What fruit do you give? I mean good fruit!!

If you are a light, you will be fruitful. Wake up and take an interest in your spiritual work. Don't you know that the Holy Bible says *"therefore every tree which does not bear good fruit is cut down and thrown into the fire"* (Matt 3:10).

Take a lesson from the earth which spins without stopping.

For thousands of years since the beginning of creation, it has been continually spinning, each turn causing one day and one night, millions of turns, without stopping!! I wonder if the earth ever tired of revolving and lazed and reclined on its axis to take a rest, would it not be entangled and confused? But through its revolutions and its continuous process of production, the earth performs the work entrusted to it by God.

Also, salt works wisely. It must not exceed or become less than the needed quantity.

If it increases it will spoil the food. If it decreases the food will not be tasty.

It is the same thing with the good guide. He must not give the people spiritual teaching above their standard in order that vanity may not tire them; or give them what is below their standard.

When David entered the battle-field he was a particle of salt and at the same time Goliath defied the ranks of Israel. David was a blessing to his people. Through him, victory and joy were accomplished. As soon as he appeared he was in charge of the situation.

Although Athanasius was a young deacon in an ecumenical council comprising of 318 Bishops, he was the salt which seasoned a whole generation: He taught people the true faith.

It was said "If not for Athanasius, the people of the world would have become Arians."

Stephen, too, was a small particle of salt, a mere deacon. He was neither a priest, a bishop, nor an apostle. He spread faith, and performed miracles "*And they were not resist the wisdom or the Spirit by which he spoke.*" (Acts 6:10).

And you, what have you done? Were you a light to others?

Salt And Light:

As salt is necessary to all, light is also necessary. The phrases "You are the salt and you are the light" mean that you are necessary for the world's benefit; not only to yourselves but also for the benefit of all human kind. Through you, faith will reach the world. Through you, people will know spiritual ways.

With your help, they will rise from their falls and return to God. Light will shine on all.

Concern yourselves then with the affairs of all people, whatever their race or colour may be.

Go to the Samaritans and the Gentiles as well as to the Jews *"Go into all the world and preach the gospel to every creature."* (Mark 16:15). Shine on all people like the sun. Don't differentiate between one and another in treatment and care.

The two words "The world" and "'The earth" mean: every place ... "You are the salt of the earth. You are the light of the world." any place you reside in, your light will shine like the sun which shines on all human beings without discrimination.

Wherever you go, people will say about you "Surely, this is one of God's sons. All will benefit from you. The place will be filled with enthusiasm and activity; and through your light, the kingdom of God will spread all over it.

The suns rays enter the palace of the king and the house of the servant and the hut of the scavenger. All are in need of these rays. All enjoy the sun's warmth and heat.

It does not discriminate between the great and the mean or between the rich and the poor. It is for all people. The sons of God also pay attention to everyone, search for all and visit the righteous as well as the evil ones.

Look at the candle. It gives light to the minister as well as the guard. Its light does not increase in the palace or decrease in the hut. It is light for all and everyone benefits from it.

May all of you learn a lesson from that candle and shine as it does in visitations, in service and in self-sacrifice.

Light purifies any place and is not contaminated by it. Light enters the chamber of the prince as well as the sheepfold without being polluted.

So if you go to sinners do not stumble as they do, but lead them to repentance.

As the sun rises on the righteous as well as on the oppressors and sends its rays to the worthy and to the unworthy, so your offer must be for all.

Your business is to give, not to condemn.

You are to be a blessing to the world as Elijah was in the house of the widow, as Joseph was in the land of Egypt, and as Abraham was a blessing to the whole world.

Light radiates without you asking it to. .

The sun does not wait for you to ask her for light, nor does the moon. Both give you light and illuminate your way without your asking.

The sons of God are the same. God has sent them to the world to give it some of the light and the good within them; even if the world does not ask them to or tries to distance itself from them. **The important thing is this: Are you light?** **Are you salt?** " *Let no one despise your youth.* " (1 Tim. 4:12).

"No-one has ever seen God." (John 1:18), but you are the image of God. People see Him in you. They love God through you, and as you are a son of God, you are in His image as you were created in His own image (Gen 1:27) .

Saint Paul, the Apostle, says " *Therefore we are ambassadors for Christ, as though God were pleading through us.*" (2 Cor 5:20).

The ambassador is the representative and the servant of his state. He cares about it.

So, too, the ambassador of Christ presents an idea about Christianity. If we act in a spiritual way, we shall give a good impression of spirituality in Christianity; but if we misbehave, we, will unintentionally injure Christianity.

Not everyone has studied Christian doctrine, but they come to know it through our life.

Many cannot differentiate between religion and adoption of a religion.

If the Christian rulers of India and South Africa had injured Christianity by their behaviour, it would be very easy for our religion to be injured through us.

When Christian men divorce their wives, even for reasons not approved by Christianity. people say "There is divorce in Christianity, and there are many things which justify it-even a mere dispute between the husband and his wife!!" while Christianity in fact does not approve of this.

God Calls Us After Himself:

The Lord is wonderful when He says "You are the light of the world."

That is because He gives us His surname and calls us after Himself.

Because He also said about Himself *"I am the light of the world. He who follows Me shall not walk in darkness."* (John 8:12).

He said "*And as long as I am in the world, I am the light of the world.*" (John 9:5).

" *The light has come into the world, and men loved darkness rather than light because their deeds were evil.*" (John 3:19).

God is the light. We are also light. What is the difference, then, between our light and God's light? **He is the true light which gives light to all people**. This is what was said about Him in the Holy Bible. (John 1:9).

It was also said about John the Baptist, who was the greatest person born of a woman (Matt 11:11) *"He himself was not the light; he came only as a witness to the light"* (John 1:8).

Yes, God is the true light and through Him we see light.

The nearer we come to God the true light, the more we shine.

This resembles the light of the sun and that of the moon.

The sun itself is light but the moon is a dark body. It receives its light from the sun.

The closer the moon is to the sun, the brighter the light reflected on it (by the sun.) is...

If the moon is at a distance from the sun, it will be a dark planet on the decline. This is observed at the end of each lunar month.

What does the Lord mean by saying "You are the light of the world?"

He wishes to say "Come near to Me in order that you may become a light, then, with the light you receive from Me, you can shine upon others."

If we behave as sons of the Lord, we shall become people of light. (Luke 16:8). Yes, *"If we walk in the light, as He is in the light,"* (1 John 1:7).

Thus, our teacher Paul, the Apostle says *"For you were once darkness, but now you are light in the Lord. Walk as children of light"* (Eph 5:8).

He also says *"You are all sons of the light and sons of the day..."* (1 Thess 5:5).

Anyone who lives in companionship with God receives God's light which overflows upon him, then he shines and people see his light.

On the spiritual side, God's light appears in his life. On the physical side, light may shine his face.

For example, the story of Moses, the Prophet: When Moses came down from the mount with the two tablets of the Covenant in his hands, his face was shining. Aaron and the Israelites were afraid to come near him. Then he put a veil over his face because of the strong light shining from it (Ex 34:30-35).

On the Mount of Transfiguration, Moses and Elijah were enveloped with a bright cloud because they were near the Lord Jesus Christ, whose light overflowed them.

Therefore live with Christ, receive light from Him. Don't pride yourself falsely in being the light of the world when you are far from the source of light.

God means by the phrase "You are the light of the world" that the more we rise in our spiritual life, the more determined and steady in faith we shall be.

On A Mount:

The Lord says "*A city on a hill cannot be hidden.*" This analogy gives us an idea about the heights which we must reach, and about the rising in spiritual life till we become like a city on a hill.

It is also in the same sermon that He says "*Therefore you shall be perfect, just as your Father in heaven is perfect.*" (Matt 5:48).

Spiritual life is an attempt to Christian perfection. As we are the image of God, we must reach the standard of this image.

If it is necessary to become the light of the world we must ascend to reach the top of the mount of spiritualities. But if you are still at the foot of the mount, climbing with difficulty, how can you be an example? And how can people see God in your life?

As for you; as long as you see that the standard is high for you; your soul will be humble. The more humble you become, the higher the Lord raises you.

This is because God gives blessing to the meek. Also, the life of humility is a light and a good example to others. The example of the mount resembles that of the candle on the stand.

But what will happen if we do not reach the top of the mount or creep at its foot?

What will happen if we turn back and lose the light inside ourselves?

What will happen if our salt loses its saltiness?

If Salt Loses Its Saltiness:

What will happen if the loses its saltiness and its prettiness? What will happen if the servant loses his effectiveness? What will happen if is no longer an example? What will happen if the lamp stand is removed from its place? (Rev 2:5).

It is an existent and probable possibility. No one is infallible. The Lord Jesus Christ mentioned this possibility. *"You are the salt of the earth. But if the salt loses its flavour, how shall it be seasoned? It is then good for nothing but to be thrown out and trampled underfoot by men "* (Matt 5:13).

The Lord Jesus Christ mentions the same possibility in regard to light and says in his sermon on the mount. *"If therefore the light that is in you is darkness, how great is the darkness!"* (Matt 6:23).

If the light which shines upon others or upon its owner is changed to darkness, where does his light come from? The eye, for example, is light and sight for its owner; if it becomes dark, will there be any other organ which can be a source of light? Will this dark eye be of any use? So it will be with you if the salt within you loses its saltiness.

What will happen if the pastors, guides and teachers are misleading?

This happened to the Jewish people and God said to them "*O My people, your guides lead you astray, they turn you from the path.*" (Is 3:12). "*For the leaders of this people cause them to err*" (Is 9:16). In the days of the Lord's incarnation and service on earth, the people's guides were wrong. With their instructions and false traditions they led the people astray. Of these we mention: the scribes, the Pharisees, the Sadducees, the priests and the elders.

What would the result be if leaders change?

The Lord says "*If the blind leads the blind, both will fall into a ditch.*" (Matt 15:14).

So the Lord called them "Blind guides." (Matt 15:14).

He also said that they shut the kingdom of heaven in men's faces (Matt 23:13) and said to them, *"You travel land and sea to win one proselyte, and when he is won, you make him twice as much as a son of hell as yourselves."* (Matt 23:15,16).

Salt will lose its saltiness if the teacher misunderstands the concept of religion and the spirituality of the commandment.

History presents us with many examples of people who were salt of the earth, and light to their generations, then they turned from the way of true faith.

- **Arius**: He was the most famous preacher of his time. He was brilliant minded and a blazing flame of intelligence. He deviated from faith and remained so until the First Ecumenical Council was held against him. He was demoted from the priesthood and was cut off from the church.

He was worthy of the Lord's words *"He is no longer good for anything, except to be thrown out and trampled by men."*.

- **Nestor and Macdonius** who were patriarchs of Constantinople.

Each of them was a head of the people and a teacher. Macdonius fell in a heresy. Thus, the Second Ecumenical Council excommunicated him. Because he also fell in heresy, Nestor was excommunicated by The Third Ecumenical Council.

Thus, they lost their dignity and their priesthood and were worthy of being trampled by men.

- **Autachy,** who was a chief and one of the most pious monks in Constantinople and who led a true ascetic life, did the same and fell in Heresy and was excommunicated by the church.

- **Origen,** who. was the most learned man of his time and the greatest theologian and one of the top men, not only in his day but along all history, fell in heresy and was also excommunicated by Pope Demetrius and by other saints and churches and councils.

There were also prophets whose salt lost its saltiness.

Ahead of those we remember:

- **Balaam**

Balaam prophesied about the Lord Christ. (Num 24:17); the Spirit of God came upon him: He was a man with a mind's eye who heard the words of God and saw divine revelations with naked eyes (Num 24:2-4), a man whom Balak, king of Moab, summoned to his country and went out to receive him; Balaam who said to Balak "*Though Balak were to give me his house all of silver and gold, I could not go beyond the word of the to do either good or bad of my own will...*" (Num 24:13).

Balaam the prophet went astray in spite of his divine revelations, prophecies and sayings.

In the Book of Revelation, God Himself gives testimony against Balaam, in the message to the angel of the church in Pergamos. The Lord gently blames him for having people who hold to the teaching of Balaam (Rev 2:14). This salt lost its saltiness and was trampled by men .

On one hand, the corruption of salt may be due to a person's thinking; on the other hand, it may be due to a person's one's behaviour. For example:

• **Samson, The Judge Of Israel:**

The Spirit of the Lord came upon Samson and began to stir him (Judg 13:25).

Through him the Lord performed miracles. He was a Nazarite, set apart to God from birth according to the prophecy of the angel of the Lord. (Judg 13:5,7). But this salt lost its saltiness for some time.

Delilah and another adulteress caused him to perish. The Lord left him. The Philistines gouged out his eyes, bound him with bronze shackles and set him to grinding in prison (Judg 16:20,21).

Samson was trampled by men; but for a time. This salt has lost its saltiness but it became salt once more. Samson's hair, the sign of his vow, began to grow again (Judg 16:22).

At the end of his days, the Lord brought deliverance through him, although he paid with his life for that deliverance.

Also, St. Paul the Apostle mentioned his name among the men of faith. (Heb 11:32).

In this field we also remember:

* **Solomon, The Wise:**

He was also the salt of the earth. The Lord appeared to him twice, in Jerusalem and at Gibeon (1 Kin 9:2). God blessed him and gave him more wisdom than all the inhabitants of the world. (1 Kin 3:12).

God spoke to him from mouth to ear. The Holy Spirit, through divine inspiration, uttered words on his lips. He wrote parts of the Holy Bible full of proverbs and wisdom.

But what happened afterwards? **The salt lost its saltiness. A tragedy took place at the end of Solomon's life.**

About this tragedy the Holy Bible says *"He had seven hundred wives princesses and three hundred concubines and his wives turned away his heart. For it was so, when Solomon was old, that his wives turned his heart after other gods, and his heart was not loyal to the Lord, his God, as was the heart of his father David. For Solomon went after Ashtoreth goddess of the Sidonians, Solomon did evil in the sight of the Lord, and did not fully follow the Lord, as did his father David. Then Solomon built a high place for Chemosh the abomination of Moab ... He did the same for all his foreign wives, who burned incense and offered sacrifices to their gods.* " (1 Kin 11:3-8).

I wonder if that salt was thrown away and trampled by men!? We have hope that God had mercy upon him.

At the end of his days, Solomon repented and wrote the Book of "Ecclesiastes" in which he said about all the worldly enjoyments he had practised *"Vanity! Vanity of vanities! All is vanity, a chasing after the wind."* (Eccl 1.2,14).

The words of God to David prove that He showed mercy to Solomon.

"I will set up your seed after you, who will come from your own body, and I will establish his kingdom."

"If he commits iniquity, I will chasten him ... But my mercy shall not depart from him, as I took it from Saul ... " (2 Sam 7:12,14,15).

Here we discern defiled salt from that which has lost both saltiness and nature.

Solomon was like the defiled salt but he kept his saltiness, the nature which loved God.

David, his father, was defiled for a time.

David, the one anointed by the Lord, upon whom the Spirit of God came and about whom the Lord said : *" `I have found*

David the [son] of Jesse, a man after My [own] heart, who will do all My will.'" (Acts 13:22).

This salt was defiled. David fell into adultery, into murder, into avenging himself upon others, and into the shedding of blood ... But God did not allow for him be thrown outside and trampled by men ... On the contrary; the Lord cleansed him until he became whiter than snow. (Ps 5 1).

Trampled By Men:

✤ The person who was trampled by men was **king Saul.**

The Spirit of God came upon him. He was anointed for God. He prophesied untill the people asked each other saying *"Is Saul, also, among the prophets?"* (1 Sam 10:10,11).

It happened that that salt lost its saltiness: He became proud; he separated himself from God; he carried his own will and took interest neither in God's will nor in the counsel of his great prophet, Samuel; and his life ended with a tragedy about which the Divine Inspiration said

"But the Spirit of the Lord departed from Saul, and distressing spirit from the Lord troubled him." (1 Sam 16:14).

Among the kinds of salt trampled by men as we have just mentioned was **Balaam the prophet, and the false teachers who came before Christ, such as Theudas and Judas, the Galdean.** (Acts 5:36,37).

199

Those men and the ones like them are the ones about whom the Lord Christ said "*All who ever came before Me are thieves and robbers, but the sheep did not hear them.*" (John 10:8).

✢.**The salt that also lost its saltiness was our father Adam and our mother Eve.**

Adam was the image of God and His likeness. The Lord created him and Eve according to His likeness. (Gen 1:26).

The Lord gave them the power to rule over the fish of the sea and the birds of the air, over the livestock and over all the creatures that move along the ground.

Adam and Eve were very pure, innocent and modest. In the generations that followed them, there was no one who could resemble them in such qualities. They did not know sin. Both of them were naked, and they felt no shame.

Then, this salt lost its saltiness. Human nature deteriorated. The Lord banished Adam and Eve from the Garden. Their offspring was downtrodden.

The serpent had authority to strike man's heel (Gen 3:15).

But God restored saltiness to the salt when he became incarnate and invoked a blessing upon our human nature and returned Adam to his original rank.

So, we have hope: when salt loses its saltiness God will restore it.

If salt becomes dirty, the Lord will purify it, and bestow upon it the reward of renewing this corrupt nature. He will not describe it as useless salt.

We have another important example:

✧ **The story of Saint Peter when he denied Christ.**

He called names, cursed and said "I don't know the man." So he committed many sins:

Fear, denying his master, paucity of faith, telling lies, cursing and denunciation.

I wonder whether, at the time, he was salt of the earth and the light of the world?

No, he was not so at that time.

However, the Lord Jesus Christ restored saltiness to him.

He did not allow this saint to be trampled by men. This happened when He restored the apostolic rank to Saint Peter and exempted him from the decision "*But whoever denies Me before men, him I will also deny before My Father who is in heaven.*" (Matt 10:33).

This is why He said to him after the resurrection "*Feed My lambs, " "Take care o My sheep.*" (John 21:15,16).

O' Lord! Have mercy on the salt which sometimes loses its saltiness and its taste.

201

The person who sometimes falls unexpectedly into human errors and slips holds his saltiness tightly and says, "*Lord, you know all things; you know that I love you.*"(John 21:17).

Deviation both in ideology and conviction makes salt lose its saltiness, as happened to the heretics and to the blind guides.

Salt also loses its saltiness through bad behaviour.

This happened to David when he committed adultery; and to Samson when he yielded to women and broke his vow, and to Balaam, whose counsel ruined the chastity and purity of the people.

The Lord forgave David and Samson but Balaam perished.

Haughtiness may make salt lose its saltiness.

At the beginning of his existence, and before he fell, the devil had been salt.

He was in the glory and brilliancy of angels, then this salt lost its saltiness when he said in his heart "I will raise my throne above the stars of God, I will make myself like the Most High (Is 14:13,14).

The result was his dismissal, along with his followers, from heaven, and he was trampled by men whom the Lord had given authority to trample on snakes and scorpions and, to overcome all the power of the enemy

The responsibility of salt for losing its saltiness increases according to the position of the one who has become salt.

The devil was an angel. This is why his losing his saltiness was a very serious matter.

So it is supposed that all those who belong to priestly or hierarchical groups must be the light of the world and the salt of the earth.

This is why the Lord said to the angel of the Church in Laodicea, "*I am about to spit you out My mouth*" (Rev 3:16).

In this way, he has been dismissed, as he is of no use for anything.

To distinguish the responsibility of each rank, the priest says when he offers the sacrifice on the altar. "*For the sake of my sins and for the sake of your congregation's ignorance.*"

His fall is a great sin and is not like the slip of all the people because "*For the lips of a priest should keep knowledge and people should seek the law from his mouth.*" (Mal. 2:7)

He cannot say "I had no idea."

For this reason, the higher a man's post is, the greater his responsibility for his sins will be; especially those who are considered examples to be followed by people, as well as teachers.

There is a great difference between a person's fall from the first floor and a fall from the tenth floor, or from a town on a hill or from a light house which shines to all people.

What is meant by ".*The salt which loses its saltiness should be thrown away?*"

Thrown Outside:

The Lord who encouraged the people and said to them "*You are the light of the world; you are the salt of the earth*" said in straightening and without partiality "*If salt loses its saltiness, it will be thrown out and trampled by men.*" **Here on earth, he will be thrown outside. There in eternity, he will also be banished.**

On earth, John the Apostle said about him "*Do not receive him into your house nor greet him*" (2 John 10).

So it happened to Demas who assisted Paul the Apostle in his service. Demas was a preacher and salt; but when he lost his saltiness he threw himself outside and separated himself from the company of believers. About him Saint Paul said, "*For Demas, because he loved this world, has deserted me.*" (2 Tim 4:10).

In such a manner, the church separated those people from its membership.

It also separated all the classes of heretics from the company of believers and all to whom the words of Paul the Apostle are applied "*But even if we or an angel from heaven preach any other gospel to you than what we preached to you, let him be accursed.*" (Gal 1: 8).

It means that he will be excommunicated from the. church and thrown outside.

The church is a group of saints and it must keep this saintliness for itself.

This meaning is quite clear in many parts of the Holy Bible.

When Saint Paul the Apostle sent his epistle to the Ephesians he directed it "*To the saints in Ephesus*" (Eph 1:1). He sent to the Philippians saying "*Greet every saint in Christ Jesus. . All the saints greet you, but especially those who are of Ceesar's household.*" (Phil 4:21,22).

He sent to the Hebrews saying "*Therefore, Holy brethren, partakers of the heavenly calling.*" (Heb 3:1). He sent to the Colossians saying "*To the holy and faithful brethren...* " (Col 1:2) and added "*Therefore, as the elect of God people, holy and beloved, put on tender mercies, kindness, humbleness of mind, meekness, longsuffering.*" (Col 3:12).

He sent to the Corinthians saying "*To the church of God which is at Corinth with all the saints who are in all Achaia*" (2 Cor 1:1). As long as the church is a group of saints she says with the singer "*Holiness adorns Your house, O 'Lord*" (Ps 93:5).

This is why only the saints entered the church, but the sinners would stand outside and beg whoever entered and whoever came out to pray for them.

The assistant deacon kept and guarded the doors of the church, and prevented the sinners who had been condemned from entering it. **With such firmness, the church maintained its holiness.**

Saint John Chrysostom prevented the empress from entering the church because she had oppressed a widow and had not been fair with her. It was of no importance to him that she was an empress. He paid no attention to the penalties that might befall him as a punishment for his daring and boldness.

Also saint Martha the contrite, gives us an idea about preventing sinners from entering the church. **Concerning this matter, the laws of the church are very clear.**

The believers are members of the body of Christ Himself. (1 Cor 6:15). Christ's members are sacred and anyone who is not sanctified cannot remain a member in Christ's body, but stays outside.

In eternity, the salt which loses its saltiness will be thrown outside.

The Holy Bible tells us about punishment in the outer darkness.

The Lord says about them "*They will be cast out into outer darkness, There will be weeping and gnashing of teeth.*" (Matt 8:12).

He also said about the servant who hid his talent in the ground, "*And cast the unprofitable servant into the outer darkness, There will be weeping and gnashing of teeth.*" (Matt 25:30).

Such people stay outside eternal paradise, away from the assembly of saints; outside the dwelling place of God and the saints; and far from the light, the light of the Lord and His saints. They remain in darkness.

The words "out" and "outside" were repeated many times when mentioning the eternal punishment.

In the parable of the Virgins, the wise went in with the bridegroom to the wedding banquet; but the foolish who had no oil in their lamps, stood outside and said "*Lord, Lord, Open to us!*"(Matt 25:11). But He replied "*I tell you the truth, I don't know you. .* "

The Lord made this matter clear; saying "*Many will seek to enter and will not be able. Once the Master of the house has risen up and shut the door, you being to stand outside and knock at the door saying Lord, Lord,, open the door for us. and he will answer, 'I don't know you ... when you see Abraham, Isaac and all the prophets in the kingdom of God, and yourselves thrust out.*" (Luke 13:24-28).

This is the story of salt which is thrown outside.

In the Bible, the Lord says about it "*Salt is good, but if the has lost its flavour, how shall it be seasoned? It is neither fit for the land nor for the dunghill, but men throw it out.*" "*He who has ears to hear, let him hear.*" (Luke 14:34,35).

CHAPTER TEN
"Let Your Light So Shine Before Men"

The Lord said "*A city that it set on a hill cannot be hidden. Nor do they light a lamp and put it under a basket. But on a lampstand, and it gives light to all who are in the house. Let your light so shine before men, that they may see your good works and glorify your Father in heaven.*" (Matt 5:14-16).

A City And A Lamp:

Here, the Lord may be speaking about the individual and the church, and how each of them is a source of light to the society and to the world.

He compares the individual or the shepherd to the lamp, and the church to the city.

He gave us light in order that it might appear before men, so they may be enlightened by it and it will guide them towards God.

This is why He said to the Jews about John the Baptist; "*John was the burning and shining lamp, and you were willing for a time to rejoice in his light.*" (John 5:35).

The believer is a night light or a lamp. He gives light to everyone in the house.

The lamp refers to God's commandments or to the one who carries it to people.

It was said in the Psalm *"The commands of the Lord are radiant, giving light to the eyes"* (Psalm 19*)*. Also *"Your word is a lamp to my feet and a light for my path."* (Psalm 119).

The words of God shed light on the spiritual way before men.

On reading the Bible in the church, we light candles as a sign of the radiation of God's words. We receive bishops with candles because they carry light to us or because they themselves are light.

For the same reason we put candles before the icons of the saints.

In Revelation, we find the same comparison in regard to the priests and to the church. It compares churches to the seven golden lampstands, and their priests to the seven stars in the right hand of the Lord (Rev 1:20).

The church is a light; the priests are light and through them, the church carries light to men.

So, it is a light and a bearer of light. As a group of believers or as a university for them, the church can be called a city as it was said about *"the Holy city, New Jerusalem, coming* *down out of heaven from God, as a bride adorned for her husband."* (Rev 21:2).

John, the Apostle said about the same city *"The city has no need of the sun or of the moon to shine in it, for the glory of God illuminated it , and the Lamb is its lamp."* (Rev 21:23).

Every luminous person can enter Jerusalem, the shining city.

"But there shall by no means enter it, anything that defiles, or causes an abomination or a lie" (Rev 21:27) because they are darkness and *"Men loved darkness rather than light because their deeds were evil."* (John 3:19).

These lights, sent by the Lord to the world, are not allowed to be hidden. Sometimes they can never be hidden.

They Cannot Be Hidden:

The city on a hill cannot be hidden.

Low and weak levels can be hidden, or at least, cannot be seen by all; but those whom the Grace of God elevated to the top cannot be hidden by any power.

For example, St. Paul the Apostle, against whom they violently waged war; whose light remained brilliant before all.

There were also the apostles to whom the high priests said *"Did we not strict command you not to teach in this name?*

211

And look, you have filled Jerusalem with your doctrine and are intend to bring guilty of this Man's blood on us." (Acts 5:28).

There were many lamps which they wished to hide under a bushel, but the Lord removed that cover to let their lights appear.

They wished to hide those lights and give them no chance to appear, either by persecuting them, or by spreading false rumours against them.

Didn't they say that the Lord Christ was a sinner because He performed miracles on the Sabbath? (John 9:24).

Didn't they say about Christ *"except by Beelzebub, the ruler of the demons."?* (Matt 12:24). Didn't they say about Him *"He is a glutton and a winebibber, a friend of tax-collectors and sinners?"* (Matt 11:19), and also that He was a Samaritan and had a devil (John 8:48)?

But all these bushels could not hide Christ's light.

How many bushels did they use to hide the light of Saint Athanasius?

How many false accusations did they charge him with? How many assemblies did they hold against him? How many times was he banished from his Episcopal seat?

In spite of all these persecutions, Athanasius remained as he had been before. The light of his instructions still shone all over the world. Indeed, he was a hero of faith.

There are many men who try to hide the shining lamp under a bushel as soon as they see it.

Evil works against the good and resists it. The devil covets the sons of God and does not wish them to be the light of the world because he himself is darkness and the supreme ruler of darkness (Luke 22:53).

This is why the devil agitates his evil followers and helpers against the believers.

They attack the faithful because of envy or jealousy or hatred for the Kingdom, or misunderstanding, or because of their inordinate desire for vainglory; or because the light of the righteous shows up their wickedness, or because of people's comparison between these and those ... or due to the continual struggle. between the kingdom of God and that of the devil.

The desire for concealment may lead to assassination.

That is, concealing changes in an action of extinguishing and making every effort to silence the sound of truth.

This is what Herod did with John, the Baptist, because the light of John showed up his sin and admonished him. (Matt 14:3-5).

Jezebel wished to do the same-thing with Elijah, the prophet. (1 Kin 19:1,2).

Also, the Empress did the same-thing with John Chrysostom who would to criticise and reprove her deeds. **The bushel may be nonfeasance and nonchalance.**

They cause talents to be idle and keep them from being employed.

Even if lights are exposed to such hindrances, God prepares for them other ranges where they illuminate far from formalities.

There were many who performed great deeds and services, although they were not officials or of great authority.

The Lord Christ himself was the true light, although He had no formal post during the period of His incarnation on earth.

Our duty is not to oppose the others' service or try to hide their light under a bushel.

Hindrance may occur through competition

It is strange to find competition in the construction of the kingdom where servants oppose each other's efforts.

Hostilities may even exist among them. Everyone tries to put a bushel over the other's work while the field of service has room enough for all. "*The harvest truly is plentiful but the labourers are few.*" (Matt 9:37).

Selfishness puts a bushel over the other person's lamp.

It does not see how wide and extended the kingdom is; but looks at the "ego" which wants to shine in the field of service. She wishes the light of her lamp to shine alone and the other lights to disappear, in order that she may remain the most outstanding personality.

There is another bushel, "Self-denial". It is hiding light under the plea of self-denial. We shall explain that subject - God willing - and begin with the Lord's words:

"Men See Your Good Deeds":

He said "Men see" and did not say "Men hear".

It is very easy for man to say good words on the outside while, the inside says the opposite.

You may hear from a person, humble sayings which shows you that he is deeply spiritual person... But if you test him in a certain way, he will become agitated and unable to put up with anything.

In this situation the words of that spirited learned person is true: **"There is a person who tell you about clouds while they welter in the mud."**

This is the reason, the Lord said "Men see your deeds." and not say "Men hear your sayings."

215

The deeds of the scribes and the Pharisees differed completely from their sayings. They did not practise what they preached and set ideals which are hard to achieve *"They bind heavy burdens, hard to bear, and lay them on men's shoulders, but they themselves will not move them with one of their finger."* (Matt 23:4).

There is a vast difference between you saying that you love a person and his or her sensation of your love and its effect on them and how they feel it through the actual dealing with them.

This is how deep the words of Saint John, the Apostle, are!!

"Let us not love with words or tongue but with action and in truth." (1 John 3:18).

Religion is not mere words or learning verses or delivering sermons but it is life and spirit.

People give light through their way of their life more than mere sayings.

Some of people's sayings are not accepted because their behaviour stand as a massive barrier against their acceptance.

There is no distance between the spiritual person and his/her deeds and sayings. .

His/her words explain deeds; and deeds are clear expression of his/her sayings. The two are similar. The important matter is that deeds must be virtuous and sensed by all people.

That leads us to an important question:

How does a view-point of a person agrees with the virtue of humility and the necessity of concealment of virtues?

Visibility And Concealment:

In many occasions the Lord explained the importance of the concealment of virtues. He says:

"Then your Father, who sees what is done in secret, will reward you." (Matt 6.-4,6, 18).

He says about the persons who display their virtues: *"I say to you the truth, they have their reward."* (Matt 6:2,5).

The Lord gives us examples about charity, prayer, and fasting.

How can we relate this meaning and His saying *"Let your light so shine before men, that they may see your good works and glorify your Father in heaven."* (Matt 5:16).

The answer to this question is concentrated in two points:

1. There are virtues which cannot be concealed.

2. There is a difference between "they may see your good works" and you perform virtues to let people see them.

You can conceal your prayer, your fastings and your charity (Matthew 6); But can you hide your truthfulness, your faithfulness and your grace when you deal with all people?

Can you hide your smooth style and your selected words which contain no defamation, no roughness and no disgrace to any-body and which do not hurt any feelings?

There are ways of behaviour which cannot be hidden as: your temper, your politeness, your personality, your wisdom, your pattern and your genteelness. All these are seen by others without any attempt from you.

If you like to hide your meekness and humility!! You will not be able to hide your quiet and gentle countenance. Can you hide your sweet and tolerant smile? Can you hide your smiling face when you meet anyone? and your peaceful and mild voice too?

Can you hide your endurance to offence and forgiving your debtors?

Can you do away with the good deed lest men should see it? Or you would rather do good deeds with your aim is not to he seen or praised by men?

The main thing is: to possess within yourself a pure heart; not to ask praise of people and to work in secrecy as far as you can and not to mention your good deeds before others.

However, you may not speak about yourself; your good deeds will speak on your behalf while you remain silent. The

good deeds speak about the Lord you worship and the religion you believe in as the heavens declare the glory of God; the skies proclaim the work of his hands. (Ps 19: 1) in complete silence or in silence which speaks loudly!!

Notice, also, that the Lord did not say *"that they may see your good deeds and praise you"* but *"that they may see your good deeds and praise your Father in heaven."*

Praise Is Due To The Lord:

Every deed you do, is done to God's glory not yours. About this matter you say with the singer, *"Not unto us, O' Lord, not unto us, but to Your name we give glory."* (Ps 115:1).

As for you yourself, you have to say as the Lord Christ said *"I do not receive honour from men."* (John 5:41).

Anything you do must be done to God and His angels. You have to say about God as the Baptist said: *"He must increase, but I must decrease."* (John 3:30).

It is enough for you that the Lord sees your good deeds but If men see them, It will be for God's glory.

The city on the hill is seen by all men without any indication from it to attract their sight. They praise the Lord who elevated it to that height. Your deeds praise God by two ways: Faith and behaviour.

People will praise God because they see His image In you and observe In you the nobleness of Christianity, and know that God's commandments can be carried out practically.

They will praise the Lord whose Grace yielded good fruit in you and brought you to such a grade of spirituality. They praise the Lord who gifted you with faith. They Will praise the Lord when they know that your good deeds are not done by your - human arm but through God's work in you and with the guidance of the Holy Spirit.

Indeed, all matters are due to God; blessed is His name in everything.

When men praise God for all these blessings, holy zeal would lead them to follow your ways and keep pace with you.

In this way, God is glorified in them. His Kingdom spreads among them through their admiration of the good deeds done by the Lord in you and through you.

This is why, anything you do, declare the part of God in it.

Instead saying to a poor person, "Take this gift." it is better to say "God has sent this sum to you. Here it is, take it." And instead of saying "At last, we could solve the problem..." say "At last, the Lord interfered into the problem and helped us to solve it."

This is why, in everything we do, whether through the body or the soul, we remember the saying of the apostle *"Therefore, glorify God in your body and in your spirit, which are God's."* (1 Cor 6:20).

Be sure that the Lord whom we praise is, not an alien , but He is our Father in heaven. The words of the Lord "Let your light shine" include a heavenly command:

A command to shine and a command to keep away any obstruction that may hide it.

It means that the Lord wishes the light to illuminate continually before men to see our good deeds and praise our Father in heaven.

And He said in the beginning *"Let there be light and there was light"* (Gen 1:3).

Also He says *"Let your light shine before men"* and this light shines before men.

God's word that goes out from His mouth will not return to Him empty (Is 55:11).

If God speaks through your tongue, the words of the Bible will be applied to you *"So the word of God spread"* (Acts 6:7).

God loves light. He said about Himself *"I have come as a light into the world, that whoever believes in Me should not abide in darkness."* (John 12:46).

As God created the sun, the moon, the stars and to illuminate the material world, so, He wishes that the spiritual lights illuminate the way before men.

This is why we should have confidence in the Lord as you are shining lights above the bushel and people can see your deeds.

Your Heavenly Father:

In the sermon on the mount, the Lord Christ concentrates on the relationship between God, as a father, and human beings.

This matter was mentioned unintentionally in the Old Testament, but, in the sermon, the Lord emphases this point.

In the sermon, the phrase "the heavenly Father" was repeated several times.

- You do good deeds that your Father in heaven may be praised (Matt 5:16).

- You pray and say *"our Father in heaven."* (Matt 6:9).

- You practise virtue in secret; then your Father will reward you. (Matt 6:4).

- You try to be perfect as your heavenly Father is perfect (Matt 5:48).

- You forgive men when they sin against you so that your heavenly Father may also forgive you. (Matt 6:14).

- You do not worry saying "What shall I eat? Or what shall I drink? For your heavenly Father knows that you need them. (Matt 6:32).

- Look at the birds of the air, ... your heavenly Father feeds them. (Matt 6:26).

- You Father in heaven gives good gifts to those who ask him (Matt 7: 11).

In the sermon on the mount, the mention of the heavenly Father is the first fruit of the Lord's teaching about this topic throughout the Bible.

The Kingdom And Heaven:

As the phrase "Your heavenly Father" is repeated several times in the sermon on the mount and throughout the Bible, there are also other phrases as:

The kingdom, heaven and kingdom of heavens.

The Lord wishes that people concentrate their thoughts on "heaven" and In "the kingdom".

In the beginning of the sermon, he says about the heavenly kingdom *"Blessed are the poor in spirit, for theirs is the kingdom of heaven."* (Matt 5:3).

It was said about the Lord Christ when He began His mission that He was *"preaching the gospel of the kingdom."* (Matt 4:23) .

The phrase *" ...preaching the gospel of the kingdom ...",* (Matt 9:35) was repeated several times and will continue till the end of the world. *"And this gospel of the kingdom will be preached in all the world as a witness to all the nations, and then the end will come."* (Matt 24:14).

"The good stands for the sons of the kingdom" (Matt 13.38), those are the believers.

"Then the righteous will shine like the sun in the kingdom of their Father." (Matt 13:43) *"and inherit, the kingdom prepared for you from the foundation of the world"* (Matt 25:34).

He who has ears, let him hear ...